Green
Pearls
of
India

Green Pearls of India

Tracing the Roots of Sacred Trees

V. Sundararaju

RUPA

Published by
Rupa Publications India Pvt. Ltd 2023
7/16, Ansari Road, Daryaganj
New Delhi 110002

Sales centres:
Bengaluru Chennai
Hyderabad Jaipur Kathmandu
Kolkata Mumbai Prayagraj

Copyright © V. Sundararaju 2023
Photos courtesy: Author Archives (unless mentioned otherwise)

P-ISBN: 978-93-5702-540-9
E-ISBN: 978-93-5702-541-6

First impression 2023

10 9 8 7 6 5 4 3 2 1

The moral right of the author has been asserted.

Printed in India

Contents

Foreword

Among Nature's creations on Earth, trees occupy a special and immense space in the heart of human beings. In the Bhagavad Gita (Chapter 15, Verse 1), Lord Krishna describes our world like a banyan tree that has different branches. The banyan tree is one of the most venerated trees in India. In Hindu mythology, the tree is often called *Kalpavriksha*, the tree that provides fulfilment of wishes and other material gains. It symbolizes Trimurti—Lord Vishnu is believed to be the bark, Lord Brahma the roots and Lord Shiva the branches. In the Ramayana, it is said that Sita sat under an Ashoka tree in Lanka. The Buddha attained nirvana sitting under a peepal tree. In our temples, there invariably exists a *sthalavriksham*, a tree unique to a specific temple, which is worshiped and venerated. Trees have had an unseen but heartfelt relationship with humans since time immemorial. We recognize, respect and even worship them in our culture and civilization because of this relationship we have developed.

In this book, V. Sundarararaju, Indian Forest Service (IFS) officer (Retd), has captured the essence and beauty of 27 trees that are sacred and are offered prayers by a large section of our people. He has vividly described the religious, social, economic, ecological, cultural and medicinal values in the most attractive manner for every reader to be interested in and benefit from.

Mr Sundarararaju has been an outstanding forest officer with great passion for nature and conservation. He has demonstrated great commitment in connecting nature and people. This book is a product of his laudable commitment towards connecting nature with people through sacred trees. In this lucidly written book, one can feel the essence of energy vibrating through the sacred trees. This excellent book is of immense value in the field of conservation of nature and is bound to enrich anyone's mind and library.

Dr C.K. Sreedharan, IFS
Former Principal Chief Conservator of Forests &
Head of Forest Forces, Chennai

Introduction

While I was in active service in the Tamil Nadu Forest Department, I could not find spare time for activities like identifying origins of sacred trees and writing articles about them. Even then, with great interest and enthusiasm, I had helped identify a 500-year-old African baobab (*Adansonia digitata*) as well as another equally old *arjuna* tree (*Terminalia arjuna*), and relevant articles had been published in *The Hindu* and the *Indian Forester* in 2006 and 2010, respectively. Ever since my retirement in 2011, I have had the opportunity to serve as a consultant for the Society for Social Forestry Research and Development Tamil Nadu, and I have been fortunate enough to travel throughout Tamil Nadu and nearby states, including Andhra Pradesh and Karnataka, for monitoring and evaluating various activities carried out by the respective state forest departments. During my evaluation work, I utilized my spare time identifying the heritage and sanctity of certain trees as a hobby. Only rare, centuries-old, strange and sacred trees are taken into account. Of course, nearly 100 trees have been identified in different parts of the state, not only within reserve forests but also outside. My articles on heritage trees have been published in various newspapers like *The Hindu*, *Indian Express*, *Times of India*, *Deccan Chronicle*, etc. I eventually turned into a blogger when I started writing for *Down To Earth*, and my scientific articles started being published periodically.

A seal dating back to 3000–4000 BCE, discovered in Mohenjodaro, reveals that the practice of tree worship is older than the Indus Valley Civilization. Worship of Hindu deities like Shiva, Ganapathy, Murugan and Vishnu is common in India. Almost every deity is attached to a sacred tree like *bael*, banyan, *kadamba, jamun* or *peepal*. While guardian deities, such as Ayyanar and Kali, are worshipped in shrines located at the entrance of many villages, the goddess connected to smallpox, Mariamman or Amman, is worshipped in almost every village in Tamil Nadu. Almost every shrine has a sacred tree like banyan, peepal or neem. A study has shown that Tamil Nadu has a notably higher concentration of banyan, peepal and neem trees that are commonly worshipped.* The naming of the villages, men, women, gods and goddesses after trees shows the auspiciousness and veneration attached to them. When trees are respected and revered by people, the affinity towards and affection for trees that develops in people knows no bounds. Because of this meaningful relationship between mankind and trees, many plants are considered sacred and worshipped all over the country. Thus, the concept of sacred trees not only helps in protection of trees but also increases tree cover through the planting of large numbers of trees, leading to mitigation of climate change, an essential service very much required in the present-day scenario.

Thus, one day, when I was contacted by Rupa Publications with a proposal to write about sacred trees, I accepted the offer immediately, and the result is this book titled *The Green Pearls of India*, which you hold in your hands. This book may evoke interest among people from different walks of life as

---

*Walter, Kurt Josef, 'Sacred Trees among the Tamil People of South India', *Suomen Antropologi*, Vol. 40, No. 1, 2016, pp. 47–65, https://tinyurl.com/2wuw8zhh. Accessed on 23 January 2023.

the trees mentioned are sacred and worshipped with great fervour and reverence throughout the Indian subcontinent by people of various religions. One may also find this book interesting because it has a lot of information on the religious and mythological value of these trees besides their cultural and ecological value.

Wood Apple (*Aegle marmelos*)

Wood Apple

Family: Rutaceae

Wood apple, also known as the bael tree, is highly venerated by Hindus. It is considered one of the most sacred trees in India. Bael is scientifically known as *Aegle marmelos* (L.) Correa ex Roxb. 'Aegle' is the Latin name for one of the Hesperides, the three sisters who, helped by a dragon, guarded the golden apples of Goddess Hera; 'marmelos' is derived from the Portuguese word '*marmelosde*' meaning 'marbled'. Its Sanskrit name, *shriphala*, means sacred fruit. This tree belongs to the Rutaceae family. It can even grow in places where no other tree can grow.

This is a glabrous and deciduous tree that grows wild in dry forests and is cultivated mostly in temple premises because of its religious value. The spiny tree with fragrant flowers grows to a height of 15 m. Its flowers are in full bloom in May and fruits appear between October and November. The grey or yellow woody fruit has a smooth outer surface and is 5–15 cm in diameter. The fruit has many seeds embedded in a thick and orange-coloured aromatic pulp. The fruit can be eaten fresh or dried and has a citrusy taste. All parts of the tree have medicinal value.

While the trade name is bael, other common names include stone apple, wood apple, Bengal quince, golden apple or Japanese bitter orange. It is called *bel* in Assamese and Bengali; *bili* in Gujarati; bel, *bilva* and *sriphal* in Hindi; *bilapartri* in Kannada; *bello* in Konkani; *marredy* and *koovalam* in Malayalam; bael in Marathi; *belo* in Odia; bilva, *vilva*, *shivadrumah,* shriphala and *tripatra* in Sanskrit; *vilvam* in Tamil; *maredu, maredi* and bilva in Telugu; and bel and *bel kham* in Urdu.

Habitat and Distribution

This tree comes up in dry and open forests on hills and plains at altitudes up to 1,200 m, with annual rainfall ranging from 570 mm to 2,000 mm. Though the bael tree is found in tropical and subtropical regions of India, it is also found in the wild in the lower Himalayan ranges up to an elevation of 500 m, growing along the foothills of the Himalayas— Uttar Pradesh, Bihar, Chhattisgarh, Uttarakhand, Jharkhand, Madhya Pradesh, the Deccan Plateau and along the eastern coastal plains. It is indigenous to the Indian subcontinent and Southeast Asia and is cultivated primarily in India, Sri Lanka, Thailand and Malaysia.

Environmental and Economic Significance

The bael tree has tremendous therapeutic and healing potential for the human body as well as the environment. Since it absorbs toxic gases from the atmosphere and makes them inert through neutralization, it acts as a 'sink' for chemical pollutants. Since bael emits a greater percentage of oxygen in the presence of sunlight as compared to some other trees, it is considered to be an air purifier. Since it is also a fragrant species, its volatile and fragrant vapours neutralize the foul smells that emanate from putrefied organic matter, make them inert and prevent bacterial infections.[*]

Bael can be cultivated commercially in waste and unproductive lands, paving the way for the economic empowerment of farmers. As the tree is drought resistant, this can be grown in Rajasthan too. The tree may take 8–10 years to yield fruits in the case of cultivation from seed. But superior quality bael has been developed through hybridization, and it may start yielding fruits after four to five years.[**] Farmers can also plant the tree along the boundary of their lands as its dense canopy may be very useful as green manure. A row of trees can serve as a windbreak if planted across the windward side of the agricultural land. The tree also acts as larval food for common Mormon and lime butterflies.

Historical Importance

Bael has been very popular in India from prehistoric times. Evidence of its religious importance is found in the Rig Veda, which states that Goddess Lakshmi, the deity of wealth and prosperity, resides in this tree. Hiuen Tsang, the Chinese Buddhist pilgrim, mentioned this tree in his account of his visit to India in the seventh century.

In Myanmar, paints are prepared traditionally by using the fruit of the tree. The extract from the tree is used for fertility control and as an antiproliferative in Bangladesh. Its parts are

---

[*]Sharma, Prabodh Chander, et al., 'A Review on Bael Tree', *Natural Product Radiance*, Vol. 6, No.2, 2007, p.172.
[**]Singh, A.K., Sanjay Singh, and P.L. Saroj, 'The Bael (Production Technology)', Technical Bulletin no. CIAH/Tech./Pub. No. 67, Director ICAR-CIAH, Bikaner. p. 18.

used in Sri Lanka for hypoglycaemic activity. There are reports about the cultivation of the tree in Northern Malaysia and Java in Indonesia, as well as the Philippines, where it yielded fruit for the first time in 1914. This species is found growing in some Egyptian gardens in Surinam and Trinidad. It was introduced in Europe in 1959. Certain specimens of bael have been introduced and maintained in the Citrus Collection in Florida, USA.

Religious and Mythological Significance

In Hindu mythology and rituals, the bael tree plays a very important role. This tree is worshipped by Hindus for multiple reasons. It is treated as the incarnation of Goddess Parvathi by many. Bael leaves are used to worship Lord Venkateswara on Fridays. Temples of Lord Murugan, Lord Vinayaka and Lord Vishnu in Tamil Nadu also consider this a sacred tree.

The bael tree is considered a form of Lord Shiva, and is cultivated in the premises of Shiva temples. The tree is also known as *shivadrumah* in Sanskrit, meaning the tree of Shiva. Many Hindus also believe that Lord Shiva lives under the tree. As the leaves are ternate (in whorls of three), they are believed to represent the three eyes or the trident of Lord Shiva, the *trimurti swaroop* (the Triumvirate of Brahma, Vishnu and Shiva) and the three syllables of sacred sound 'Om'. The bael tree is considered one of his favourite trees, as he is said to be fond of its leaves and fruits. Thus, bael leaves and fruits play a prominent role in the worship of Lord Shiva. It is said that the one who worships Shiva Linga under the bael tree will be blessed to reach the abode of Lord Shiva.

As the front tip of the leaf supposedly contains nectar, it must face the statue of the god while being offered. In fact, another name of Shiva is Bilvadandin, which means holder of a bilva-wood staff. Six Shiva temples in Tamil Nadu have gods named after this tree. The famous saint-poet Thirugnana Sambanda, one of the three celebrated Nayanmaars of the sixth century and a Shiva devotee, mentioned the importance of this tree in Thevaram, a collection of Tamil devotional poetry dedicated to Lord Shiva. 'Bilwashtakam', one of the hymns of Lord Shiva, considered to be a powerful mantra, discusses the bael tree:

Tridalam trigunakaaram trinethram cha triyayusham,
Trijanma papa samharam eka bilwam sivarpanam.

[I offer one leaf of bilva to Lord Shiva,
Which has three leaves,
Which causes three qualities,
Which are like the three eyes of Shiva,
Which is like the triad of weapons,
And which destroys sins of three births.]

Bilwashtakam idham punyaam, padeth Shiva sannidhou
Sarva papa nirmuktha Shiva loka maapnuyath.

[Reading this holy octet of bilva,
In the presence of Lord Shiva,
Would save one from all sins,
And in the end take him to the world of Shiva.]

∾

Bael tree of Lord Shiva: In Indian mythology, the bael tree is associated with the star Chiththirai, one of the stars in the almanac. The trifoliate leaves are considered the seat of Brahma (the Creator), Vishnu (the Sustainer) and Shiva (the Saviour). The tree is also known as *mangalya* and *atimangalya*, meaning auspicious, as well as shriphala or fruit of the goddess. It is also called *syandilya* (removing illness); *sailush* (beautiful fruit-bearing tree widely distributed in mountainous regions); *maloor* (helps to increase skin complexion); *gandha garbha* (seat of smell); *kandaki* (thorns); shivadrumah (tree of Lord Shiva); *sadaphala* (fruit in abundance); *sathyaphala* (fruit with positive energy) and *peethaphala* (yellow-coloured fruit).

Goddess Lakshmi has close association with the tree as well. She has been depicted in the Bhuvanesvari Tantra with a bilva fruit in her lower left hand. Moreover, according to Tantric folklore, Goddess Lakshmi had once come down to Earth in the form of a cow. It is said that the bilva tree had arisen from the dung of this sacred cow. Another tale of Goddess Lakshmi's association with the bael tree is described in the Brihatdharma Purana. Goddess Lakshmi, in her worship of Lord Shiva, used to offer a thousand lotus flowers, plucked by her handmaids, every day. One day, there were two less than a thousand. Lakshmi believed it to be inauspicious to offer anything less than a thousand. At that time, she remembered that Lord Vishnu, her husband, had once described her breasts as blooming lotuses. So, she decided to offer them in place of the two missing flowers. Lakshmi cut off one breast and placed it on the altar with the flowers. When she attempted to cut off the other breast, Shiva, who was extremely moved by her devotion, appeared before her and stopped her. He then reshaped her cut breast into the sacred bael fruit, which was then sent to Earth to flourish near his temples. Because of the close connection between bael and Goddess Mahalakshmi, worshipping her on Fridays by offering bael leaves is said to be auspicious. The devotional hymn given below from Sri Suktam (Hymns of Goddess Lakshmi) discusses the bilva tree.

[I surrender myself to You, O resplendent like the Sun!
By your power and glory, trees like the bael have grown
up, may the fruits thereof destroy through the grace of all
inauspiciousness rising from the inner organs and ignorance
as well from the outer senses.]*

Bael is revered as a sacred tree in more than 198 temples in Tamil Nadu, including the temples in Thiruvaiyaru, Thiru Erumbiyur and Thiru Rameswaram. Vasuman, the king of Videhas, is believed to have regained his lost kingdom by going around the bael tree at the temple of Thiruvidaimarudur in Tamil Nadu.

Apart from Tamil Nadu, in Rajasthan, Rajput kings perform the ceremony of worshipping the bael tree, considered the most sacred of Dussehra rites, on the seventh day of the festival. A bael fruit is picked fresh from the tree and offered to the fierce Goddess Chamundi to invoke her protection. In West Bengal, Goddess Durga is aroused from her sleep during Durga Pooja by the touch of a twig from a bael tree growing in the northeasterly direction. Once awake, the goddess is supposed

---

*'Aswapti's Yoga-Tapasya: Hymns to the Goddess', *Savitri*, https://tinyurl. com/275he8pp. Acessed on 02 August 2023.

to take up her abode in the tree. As a part of Bel Bibaaha, a ritual celebrated in the Hindu and Buddhist religions by the Newar people of Nepal, prepubescent girls are married to the bael fruit as a symbolic gesture to safeguard against the social stigma endured by widows in their community. This is done so that if the husband were to die later in her life, she was to not be considered a widow, thus possibly dodging the *sati-pratha*. Moreover, offering bael leaves to Lord Shiva during the Mahashivaratri festival is considered highly auspicious, and it is believed that Shiva's worship cannot be completed without offering bael leaves.

Auspiciousness of Mahashivaratri: Once, there was a hunter named Gurudruh who lived in Varanasi. He did not go to temples or observe any rituals as he did not believe in God. One day, he went to the forest to hunt. As the night fell, he climbed over a bael tree growing near a pond and waited to hunt the animals that came there to quench their thirst. It happened to be an auspicious day, Mahashivaratri, and there was a Shiva Linga under the tree. Since Gurudruh had waited for the whole night without any sleep, he incidentally started plucking the bilva leaves one by one and dropped them on the Shiva Linga. Lord Shiva was pleased by the offering of the bael leaves and transformed the cruel hunter into a knowledgeable person and blessed him to attain moksha on an auspicious day.

There have been mentions of the tree in ancient Indian scriptures like the Vedas, Puranas such as the Yajur Veda, and the Mahabharata. The Skanda Purana says that the bael

Wood Apple leaves in Kasavanahalli Bangalore
Shot by Ajit, https://tinyurl.com/2rjcecke

tree originated from the sweat of Goddess Lakshmi, which fell on Mount Mandra. It is believed that the tree emits positive frequencies and eliminates negative energies when a person comes close to it. The bael tree is also venerated in Vastu Shastra. According to Vastu, it is strongly believed that if a house has the tree in the northeast, it will be blessed with wealth and remove unforeseen dangers; if in the east, the house will be blessed with happiness, peace and good health; if in the west, the house will be bestowed with health and progeny; and if in the south, the house will be protected from troubles caused by Yama.

It is believed that the presence of a bael and a *ber* (jujube) tree together indicates an underground spring. There is also a common belief that if people worship the bael tree by going around it before starting a new venture, they will be blessed by the tree. Planting the tree along the wayside is also believed to provide a long life to the one who has planted it.

Usage

The tender leaves are used in salads. The leaves are also used to obtain essential oil. The twigs and leaves are used as fodder for cattle. The juice obtained from the leaves can be applied over the body before taking a bath, as they are scented. The twigs of the bael tree are also used as toothbrushes. Sweet, flavoured water is distilled from its flowers. The nutritious, tasty and aromatic pulp of its fruit is used for preparation of *sharbat* or squashes during summer because of its sweet and pleasant taste. Bael fruit is used for preparation of candy, powder and other eatables. The gum-like substance found around the seeds can be used as adhesive. It can be used as varnish as well, and adds brilliance to water-colour paints. The yellow dye obtained from the unripe rind is used with myrobalan in calico printing. The shell of the fruit is used to add sweet odour to hair oil in Thailand. An essential oil known as marmelle oil is distilled from the rind. The bael fruit is commonly consumed during breakfast in Indonesia. The pulp of the fruit mixed with lime is used for strengthening mortar and is also used as cement for construction of wells. The pulp is used as a substitute for soap for washing clothes. It can also be used for making pickles. The dried fruits, after removal of the pulp from the rind, are used as boxes for storing medicine, sacred ashes and snuff balls. The inedible gum obtained from the stem is used for book binding. The tree is considered as a suitable windbreak or wind barrier. The wood, which takes a fine polish, is utilized for building houses, carts, and agricultural implements, carving, making pestles for oil and sugar mills, naves of wheels, tool handles, combs, etc.

The tree parts are mentioned in ancient systems of medicine. Almost all parts of the tree—leaf, fruit, seed, bark and root—have played a key role in the preparation of numerous medicinal formulations. This is considered one of the most useful medicinal trees in India because of its curative properties. In traditional systems of medicine, it has been used to treat diarrhoea, dysentery, constipation, peptic ulcer and gynaecological disorders. The leaves are used to treat diabetes, peptic ulcer, jaundice, leucorrhoea, wounds, deafness, conjunctivitis, gastric problems, irritation in the bowl, paediatric disorder, etc. The extract obtained from the flowers can be used to treat dysentery and diabetes. A tonic prepared from the flowers is used to treat epilepsy. The juice of the fruit is used to treat constipation and dyspepsia. The fruits are used to treat viral and intestinal parasites, tuberculosis, gynaecological disorders, urinary complaint, blood sugar, intestinal disorder, piles, ulcer, diarrhoea, dysentery and irritation in the elementary canal. The roots are used to treat diarrhoea, snake bite and inflammation. As the products of bael are known for curative and therapeutic values, they have become popular even in the international market.

Bael, a Divine Tree: About 170 temples of Lord Shiva have been named after the bael tree in Tamil Nadu. Four temples of Lord Muruga, one temple of Lord Vinayaga and 25 temples of Lord Vishnu are named after the tree in the state. Around 10

villages have been named after this tree in Tamil Nadu. There are about six villages named after this tree in the states of Gujarat, Maharashtra and Andhra Pradesh.

Cultivation Practices

Generally, farmers are advised to use planting material produced through vegetative propagation, as the trees grown from seeds may bear fruits only after 8–10 years. Before the onset of monsoon, pits of 1m × 1m × 1m size can be dug up at an espacement of 4–5 metres. The seedling is planted in the middle of the pit and support is provided. Watering is needed to establish the younger trees. Budded and grafted trees may start yielding fruits after four to five years of planting. The fruits may take about a year to ripen. A matured tree (10 years old) of budded or grafted variety may produce about 150–200 fruits, if it is managed properly. The fruits can be stored for two weeks at normal temperature.

Pant Aparna, Pant Shivani, Pant Sujata, Pant Urvashi, Narendra Bael-5, Narendra Bael-7, Narendra Bael-9, CISH B-1, CISH B-2 and Goma Yashi are some improved varieties produced via vegetative propagation in agricultural universities and Indian Council of Agricultural Research (ICAR) institutions. G.B. Pant University of Agriculture and Technology, Pantnagar, Uttarakhand; Narendra Dev University of Agriculture and Technology, Faizabad, Uttar Pradesh; Central Institute of Sub-Tropical Horticulture, Lucknow, Uttar Pradesh; and Central Horticultural Experiment Station, Godhra, Gujarat, may be approached for procurement of the improved tree varieties and for obtaining technical advice on planting and management of the trees on a large scale.

Jackfruit (*Artocarpus heterophyllus*)

Jackfruit

Family: Moraceae

According to the Greek historian Theophrastus, the Jack tree has been known in parts of India since 300 BCE. Botanist Ralph Randles Stewart suggests that this tree was named after William Jack, a Scottish botanist who worked for the East India Company in Bengal, Sumatra and Malaya. In Latin, this is known as *Artocarpus integra* (Thunb.) Merr. and *Artocarpus integrifolia* Linn. Jackfruit is the national fruit of Bangladesh and Sri Lanka. In India, this is the state fruit of Kerala and Tamil Nadu.

The Jack tree is known by different names: the trade name is Jack, while jackfruit is the English name. Locally, its names are *kamdal* in Bengali; *phanas* in Gujarati; *kathal* in Hindi; *halasu* and *alasa* in Kannada; *pilavu* in Malayalam; *phanas* in Marathi; *panasa* in Sanskrit; *pala* and *pila* in Tamil; and *panasa* in Telugu.

This is a large, evergreen tree with a short bole and dense crown. It grows in the evergreen forests of the Western Ghats at an altitude of 450–1,200 m. Sometimes it develops buttress roots. Inflorescences containing thousands of flowers are formed on the trunk, branches and twigs. Both male and female flowers are found on the tree. Flowering occurs between December and March. Fruiting takes place during April–June. The multi-fruit formed from a cluster of flowers, or inflorescence, is ellipsoid or round. It may have about 100–500 seeds. The fruit is aromatic and delicious.

Habitat and Distribution

The origin of this tree is considered to be in the region between the Western Ghats of southern India to the rainforests of Borneo. The jackfruit tree is also suited to tropical lowlands. Its fruit is the largest tree-borne fruit, weighing a maximum of 55 kg. A mature tree can produce about 100–200 fruits annually. This tree is cultivated extensively throughout the tropical regions of the world. Malaysia, Philippines, Cambodia and Sri Lanka are the nations engaged widely in the cultivation of jackfruit.

Religious Significance

The jackfruit is considered as one of the auspicious trio of fruits in Tamil Nadu: mango, Jack and banana (*mambazham*, pala and *vaazhai*—a trio known as *mukkani*). In Kerala, the Hindus use a wooden plank made of this tree as the priest's seat during religious rituals. Jack wood is used for making Buddhist statues in temples in Vietnam. It is also used to kindle sacred fire. The light-brown dye obtained from the heartwood of this tree is used to dye the robes of Buddhist monks in Southeast Asia. The leaves are designed into attractive eco-friendly disposable spoons to drink/eat rice gruel with green gram curry in Kerala. It has various local names including *kandakiphal* (fruit covered with thorns), *atibrihatphal* (extra-large fruit) and *amasayaphal* (fruit in the shape of stomach).

In Manipur, the sacred jackfruit tree, situated on the hill of Kaina, is an archaeological and historical site as declared by the Archaeological Department of Manipur. Renowned images

A jackfruit tree laden with fruits
Shot by Biju Karakkonam, https://tinyurl.com/4dta94ad, licensed under CC BY-SA 4.0

of Lord Krishna were carved out of this tree. There is an interesting lore associated with the carving of the images. The story goes that Bhagya Chandra, the king of Manipur in the eighteenth century, received instructions from Lord Krishna in his dream to carve the images from the tree and, accordingly, seven images were carved and installed in different places in Manipur as well as in the neighbouring state of Assam. The location of the jackfruit tree is a religious and historical site for the Meitei Hindus. When Chandra's uncle plotted with the Burmese king to oust him from Manipur, Chandra was ordered by the Assamese king to fight with a rogue elephant to prove his bravery. Since Chandra was a very religious person and a devotee of Lord Krishna, on his appeal, Lord Krishna appeared in the form of a rogue elephant in front of the jackfruit tree in Kaina and bowed before him instead of attacking him. Then, with the support of the Assamese king, Chandra led an army and regained his kingdom.

There are 30 temples in Tamil Nadu wherein the jackfruit tree is worshipped as a sacred tree. Out of these, 22 temples are of Lord Shiva, seven temples are of Lord Vishnu and one is of Lord Hanuman. About 20 villages in Tamil Nadu are named after this tree. In states like Andhra Pradesh, Bihar, Gujarat, Karnataka, Kerala, Maharashtra, Madhya Pradesh, Rajasthan and Uttar Pradesh, close to 16 villages have been named after this tree. Various proverbs and puzzles have been developed in Tamil using the Tamil name of the jackfruit. This tree is mentioned by different names in Tamil literature by famous poets like Kabilar, Thirumoolar, Uruththirankannanaar, Thiruththakka Thevar, Ilanaaganaar, Baranar, etc. Men in Tamil Nadu are commonly named after this tree too.

Mythological Significance

In Indian mythology, the jackfruit tree is associated with the star Uthiradam, one of the stars in the almanac.

There is an interesting story of the jackfruit tree involving Lord Shiva and Goddess Parvathi. Once, Lord Shiva happened to meet a beautiful tribal girl called Koolivaka while on a hunt in the forests. He became lustful because of the solitude of the forest and the beauty of the girl; he informed her of his desire and told her to wait until his return from his hunting expedition. Since Koolivaka was a staunch devotee of Parvathi, she was unwilling to participate and thus prayed to the goddess to save her from this predicament. Pleased with her piety and innocence, Parvathi revealed that in her previous birth, Koolivaka had been known as Manaswini and had been a servant in the goddess's retinue. She had happened to breastfeed Vinayaka, Parvathi's child. Upon seeing this, Goddess Parvathi had become angry and cursed her to be born in a family of outcastes. However, when she had calmed a little, Parvathi had granted a boon to her to breastfeed the son of Shiva in her next birth. After hearing Koolivaka's plea, Parvathi decided to take her form. She waited for Lord Shiva by swinging on a creeper attached to a jackfruit tree. Thus, Goddess Parvathi deceived Lord Shiva in the form of Koolivaka, and their union resulted in a son named Chathan. Koolivaka was given the responsibility of raising this divine child. After a few years, Chathan started on his journey to Kailash on the buffalo given by Lord Shiva for his protection. As he realized that Nandikeshwara would not allow him to enter Kailash in his present form, he took the form of Lord Vishnu. At that, Shiva and Parvathi recognized their son and hugged him out of happiness. Lord Shiva blessed him to be known as Vishnumaya. Subsequently, Chathan challenged the asura Jalandhara and defeated him. After winning the battle, Chathan returned to his home to live with the poor and provide protection to them.

Usage

The leaves of the jackfruit tree are used to wrap food items. They are fastened together to make disposable plates. Tender jackfruit leaves and young male flower clusters are cooked and eaten. Young leaves are used as fodder for cattle and other livestock. The fruit is the most valuable and edible part of the tree. When the fruit is ripe, it can be eaten raw; when it is unripe, it can be cooked. Both the fruit and seeds are cooked and eaten. Chips, *papad*, candy, jam, ice-cream, etc. are prepared from ripe jackfruit. The wood of the jackfruit tree is used to make furniture, musical instruments, boats, turnery and brush-backs, as well as for building construction. A yellow dye, obtained by boiling sawdust or chips of wood in water and fixed by alum, is used for colouring cloth, especially to dye the robes of Buddhist monks in Myanmar. The bark yields a gum. The juice is used as birdlime. Roots of old trees are used for carving or to make picture frames. In coastal regions, dried branches are used to produce fire by friction in religious ceremonies.

There are several medicinal uses of the jackfruit. It is nutritious, cool, delicious and prevents excessive formation of bile. It strengthens the body and increases virility. The fruit is non-carcinogenic and helps in lowering blood pressure. The extract from its seed, root and bark is used to treat diarrhoea and dysentery. The root extract is used to treat skin disease, asthma and fever. The heated leaves of this tree are used to heal wounds. The ash of the bark is used to treat abscesses and ear problems. The ash of the leaves mixed with coconut oil is used to heal ulcers. The bark of matured tree is used to release the placenta after calving in cows. Its decoction and latex are used to treat asthma, ringworm and cracks in the feet. The infusion of mature leaves and bark is used to treat diabetes, gallstones and asthma. The leaves also play an important role in healing wounds, treating pain and resolving ear problems.

Cultivation Practices

Generally, seeds are gathered from ripe fruits. Shade-dried seeds should be sown within a few days. Germination can be enhanced by soaking the seeds in water for 24 hours. Seedlings are to be planted in 1 m × 1 m × 1 m size pits. Spacing varies from 8 m to 12 metres. Watering is to be provided once a week till the saplings take root. As the tree is sensitive to drought, irrigation during dry periods is essential for better growth. The tree starts yielding from the fifth year when grafted and eighth year in case of seed origin. Normally, a jackfruit tree at its peak bearing stage may yield up to 250 fruits annually. The weight of the fruit may be up to 50 kg.

Neem/Margosa (*Azadirachta indica*)

Neem or Margosa

Family: Meliaceae

The margosa tree, scientifically known as *Azadirachta indica* A. Juss belongs to the Meliaceae family. The trade name of this species is neem. This is also called *nimgachh* in Bengali; neem in Gujarati and Hindi; *hebbavu* in Kannada; *veppu* in Malayalam; *limba* in Marathi; *nimba* in Sanskrit; *vembu* and *veppam* in Tamil; and *vepa* in Telugu.

Neem is a large, handsome, fast-growing and long-lived evergreen tree with a wide-spreading, dense and ovoid crown. This can grow up to about 15 m tall. The trunk is short and straight with a bitter bark. This tree flowers in March–May and fruiting occurs in July–August. It is found in dry forests, and is also planted along avenues in areas of human habitation. This tree thrives on black cotton soil and is adaptable to various habitats.

Habitat and Distribution

Neem grows almost anywhere in the lowland tropical and subtropical regions. It is cultivated at altitudes up to 1,500 m, but growth is considered to be very good when below 700–800 m. This species prefers soil with good drainage. The established trees can withstand drought. Neem is a good coppice tree. It is native to the Indian subcontinent, that is, India, Bangladesh, Maldives, Nepal, Pakistan and Sri Lanka. Neem trees also grow in islands located in the southern part of Iran. Following its reputation as a reliever of sickness, neem was introduced a century ago in tropical Africa, South America and Central America.

Historical Significance

The Siddha medical system originated in Tamil lands. The system is believed to have originated with the Dravidian civilization between 10,000 and 4000 BCE in the ancient island of Kumari Kandam, which now lies submerged in the sea. The medicinal knowledge is said to have come from the Siddhars, or the enlightened ones. Agasthiyar Gunavagadam, a Siddhar, is said to be the father of Siddha medicine. His description of many remedies that use neem to cure and treat a wide range of diseases can be found in 350-year-old palm leaf manuscripts. Agasthiyar prescribes neem flowers to treat bile disorders, leaves for ulcers and bark for psychiatric disorders.

The ancient Indus Valley Civilization, existing roughly between 2600 and 1800 BCE and rediscovered at the beginning of the last century, disclosed the first strong evidence of the medicinal use of neem for smallpox and chickenpox, long before any written reports.

The earliest authentic report of the curative properties of neem and its uses in the indigenous system of medicine in India is found in Kautilya's Arthashastra, written around fourth century. The Upavana Vinoda, an ancient Sanskrit treatise of the second century, which deals with forestry and agriculture, reports neem as a cure for ailing soils, plants and livestock. The Brihat Samhita of the Varahamitra (sixth century) recommends planting of neem near residential areas to stave off smallpox and chickenpox. Knowing the beneficial properties of neem, Unani scholars named it as *Shajar-e-Munarak* or The Blessed Tree. Persian scholars call neem *Azad Dirakht-I-Hind*, bearing the meaning of the Noble or Free Tree of India.

The Neem Patent Case: In 1994, the European Patent Office (EPO) granted a patent for the use of anti-fungal agents derived from neem to the United States Department of Agriculture and the multinational W.R. Grace. A global coalition of environmental groups challenged the patent, claiming that the process had been in use in India for more than 2,000 years. In 2000, when the EPO revoked the patent, ruling in favour of India, W.R. Grace appealed, claiming that no report had ever been published in any scientific journal about it. But after considering the detailed report made by the legal opposition about the traditional use of neem derivatives over thousands of years to cure colds, flu, malaria, skin diseases and even meningitis with relevant supporting data, the appeal was dismissed. Thus, the legal battle helped establish the intimate traditional and cultural association the people of India have with neem.

Religious Significance

Neem is worshipped as sacred in about 40 temples in Tamil Nadu. About 90 villages have been named after this tree in that state. In states like Andhra Pradesh and Kerala, about 20 villages have been named after this tree. More than a dozen proverbs and many puzzles using the name of this tree have been developed in Tamil. This tree has been described by Tamil poets using names like *baranar, ilangovadikal, ilankeeranaar, kovoorkizhaar, nakkeeranaar, paranjothi munivar, saththanaar, thirumoolar*, etc. in Tamil literature. Men are commonly named after this tree.

A small quantity of neem leaves and jaggery is consumed on Ugadi, the new-year festival, in Andhra Pradesh, Telangana and Karnataka to indicate that one should accept both bitter and sweet things in life. A cold broth-like concoction made with neem flowers, known as Ugadi pachhadi, is very popular in Andhra Pradesh, Karnataka and Telangana. In Maharashtra, people drink a small amount of neem juice before starting the celebrations of the new-year festival called Gudi Padva. Neem leaves play a very important role in the thousand-year-old tradition of the Mariamman temple festival in Tamil Nadu in the summer months of April–June every year. In the festival, the statue of Goddess Mariamman is garlanded with neem leaves and flowers. During festivals and weddings, the people of Tamil Nadu adorn their surroundings with neem leaves and flowers not only as a form of decoration but also to ward off evil spirits and infections. The people of Tamil Nadu strongly believe that diseases like pox and measles could be cured only by neem leaves and with the blessings of Goddess Mariamman. In the coastal state of Odisha, the famous Jagannath temple deities are made of neem heartwood along with some essential oils and powders.

Mythological Significance

In Sanskrit, neem is also called *arishta*, meaning 'perfect, complete and imperishable' because of its powerful healing powers.

According to legend, the origin of the neem tree is associated with the captivating tale of Palazhimadhanam, the churning of the mythological ocean of milk, Palazhi. During this churning, Lord Dhanvanthari emerged from the ocean carrying a pot filled with the celestial nectar known as amrit, the elixir of immortality. Amidst a struggle, Lord Indra, the king of devas, cleverly managed to seize the pot from the asuras and returned to Devaloka (heaven). Along the way, a few precious drops of the nectar accidentally fell on Earth, and it is believed that the neem tree sprouted from these divine droplets. Neem is revered as a manifestation of Neemari Devi, the Mother Goddess (Kali or Durga). It is believed that Goddess Mariamman embodies the divine essence of the neem tree, wielding its leaves like a powerful sword to combat diseases and illnesses.

In the epic Ramayana, neem holds a significant place as one of the ten trees in the Nandavanam. The tree finds mention in various ancient texts including the Mantra Maharnavam, Brihat Samhita, Kadambari, and Padma Purana. Its importance is also documented in the Charaka Samhita, a renowned medical treatise dating back to 2000 BCE.

According to Hindu Puranic legends, during a time of conflict with the asuras, the devas sought shelter by taking refuge in different trees. Lord Shiva is said to have concealed himself in the bael tree (*Aegle marmelos*), Lord Vishnu in the banyan tree (*Ficus benghalensis*), Lord Indra in the sireesha

Olive-like fruits of the neem tree

tree (*Albizzia lebbeck*), and Lord Surya (the Sun God) sought asylum in the protective embrace of the neem tree.

Usage

As neem has insect-repellent qualities, its dried leaves are used as mothballs in clothes and books. Neem contains the principal active compound azadirachtin, which is a potent insect repellent. Though every part of the tree has this compound, the highest concentration is found in the seeds. Neem seeds are used in the preparation of effective organic pesticide. The seed oil is used for oiling the hair and scalp, in lamps, for soaps, cosmetics, pharmaceuticals, etc. Resin obtained from the trunk is used for making soap, toothpaste and skin lotions. People have used neem twigs as toothbrushes since time immemorial which helps strengthen the gums. The wood is used for construction and to make furniture. Neem trees are generally grown along the roadside in dry and arid places as they purify the environment.

In the Ayurvedic medical system, neem is considered as a panacea for a number of ailments. Every part of the tree has medicinal use. Neem is used to clear toxins from the body, reduce inflammation, lower fever, promote healing and improve body function. Neem leaf teas are used to treat malaria, peptic ulcers and intestinal worms. The leaf juice is applied externally for treating ulcers, wounds, boils and eczema. The oil obtained from the seeds is applied externally in case of leprosy. A decoction of the bark is applied externally to haemorrhoids. Because of its bitter taste, neem pacifies *pitta* and *kapha dosha*. Therapeutically, this is used against fever, hyperacidity, excessive mucous secretion, vomiting, thirst, diabetes, poisonous bites, malaria, chicken pox, etc.

Economic Significance

Neem can be raised in waste lands owned either by the government or privately. It can be planted in lands that are not fit for cultivation, along the roadsides and on stream banks. As there is a heavy demand for neem products such as seeds, oil and cakes, its cultivation can bring good revenue. In villages, elderly women can have considerable earnings through collection of its fruits. The seeds, oil and cakes of neem are used as organic pesticides in agriculture for increased and disease-free yield. Farmers can have additional income by planting neem trees in barren lands. They can also be planted in a row as windbreak.

Neem trees purify the air by neutralizing toxic gases and filtering dust particles. They also kill many insects in the atmosphere. Large-scale planting of neem could be beneficial in mitigating the impact of toxic gases produced by industrial complexes. Planting this tree near residential areas helps to ward off measles, smallpox and chickenpox.

Cultivation Practices

Up to 90 per cent germination is expected with fresh neem seeds; germination takes place within a week's time. Around 10-cm-tall seedlings can be transplanted into containers; about 30-cm-tall saplings can be planted in 30 cc pits at a distance of 3 m × 3 m. Watering is needed initially for better establishment of the trees. The trees start bearing fruits after four to five years. After 10 years, the trees will bear fruits regularly.

Neem, a Germ Killer: Neem has been referred to as a 'germ killer' since ancient times. As it is believed to kill atmospheric germs, invariably, it is grown in the courtyard of most houses. Patients suffering from chickenpox are made to lie down on a bed of neem leaves and bathe in water boiled with them.

When someone suffers from chickenpox, it is customary to hang bunches of neem leaves in front of the house in order to caution the visitors of the contagious disease.

∼

Red Silk-Cotton (*Bombax ceiba*)

Red Silk-Cotton

Family: Bombacaceae

The red silk-cotton tree is a very large, often buttressed, deciduous tree with whorled branches having sharp conical prickles spreading almost horizontally. It grows to a height of 20 m, but old trees up to 60 m have been observed in wet tropical regions. The trunk and the limbs of the tree bear many conical spines, but these disappear as it becomes older. The leaves are palmate with about six leaflets radiating from a central point. Cup-shaped flowers, solitary or clustered, usually dark-crimson or scarlet, appear in December–January. The fruit is light green when raw and turns brown as it ripens. This tree also produces a capsule, which, when ripe, contains white fibres like cotton. Its seeds are numerous, ovoid and black or grey in colour.

This tree belongs to the Bombacaceae family. The scientific name of the tree is *Bombax malabaricum* DC. 'Bombax' means silkworm in Greek and 'malabaricum' denotes that the tree comes from Malabar. The current name is Bombax ceiba L. One of its heterotypic synonyms, *salmalia*, bears etymological resemblance to the Sanskrit name *shalmali*, which has been a very familiar name of this tree in India since ancient times. It is believed that Pitamaha or Brahma rested under this tree after he created the world. The cup-like flowers of the tree are considered sacred to Lord Shiva. When the tree is in full bloom, it is compared to Lakshmi, the goddess of good fortune. Countries like Bangladesh, China,

Laos and Portugal have released stamps bearing the flowers of shalmali.

The trade name of shalmali is *semal*. It is also known by different names in different languages: *ximolu* in Assamese; *shimul* and shalmali in Bengali; *raktashimul* and *sawar* in Gujarati; semal and *raktasimul* in Hindi; *burga* and *pula* in Kannada; *ilava* and *elavam* in Malayalam; *tera* in Manipuri; *savar* and *kate savar* in Marathi; shalmali and *yamadruma* in Sanskrit; *Elavamaram, ilavu, malai-elavam* and *mul-ilavam* in Tamil; and *baruga* and *baruya* in Telugu. In the book *The Useful Native Plants of Australia* written in 1889, the tree was termed *Bombax malabaricum* and its common names, simool tree or Malabar silk-cotton tree of India. As the tree has thorns on its trunk, it has also earned the name *kantakadruma* (prickly tree).

Habitat and Distribution

Red silk-cotton is a tropical tree found growing in deciduous forests up to an altitude of 1,500 m and occasionally in open country. Though native to India and Myanmar, this tree is also widely planted in Southeast Asian countries like Vietnam, Malaysia, Indonesia, southern China and Taiwan. This tree was introduced in China in the 200 BCE, according to Chinese historical records. It is extensively planted in parks and along the roadsides for its beautiful red flowers. It does not grow to its full height in semi-arid climates but is found in dense population all over Northeast India due to its subtropical climate and heavy rainfall. This tree is found in eastern parts of Pakistan as well.

Ecological Significance

Red silk-cotton trees are pollinated by birds, bats and bees when they visit the flowers to drink nectar. Birds like black drongo, bank myna, Indian myna, jungle myna, jungle crow, house crow, tree pie, red-whiskered bulbul, etc. visit the flowers during the daytime between 6.00 a.m. and 6.00 p.m. Bats, including the great Indian fruit bat, the greater short-nosed fruit bat and the long-winged tomb bat, visit the flowers from 7.00 p.m. to 4.00 a.m. The bees that visit the flowers are the Asiatic honeybee, the dwarf honeybee and the carpenter bee. As this tree is very large with wide spreading branches, it provides suitable cover for roosting and resting for a large number of birds, including vultures. Since the trees are exploited commercially, the availability of the trees has declined sharply, leading to decline in population of birds, especially vultures. The ban imposed on felling, transportation and export of this tree in Nepal since 1999 has not only helped to conserve this tree species but also critically endangered birds like the white-backed vulture and the Bengal vulture.

Mythological Significance

There are interesting mythological stories associated with the shalmali tree. Shalmali finds many mentions in Hindu mythology, especially in the Mahabharata. Once, Yudhishthira sought Bhishma's counsel on how a feeble, insignificant and timid person, provoked by someone's speech and relying on his strength, should respond when facing a formidable enemy filled with rage, determined to annihilate him. Bhishma described the following discourse that took place between a shalmali tree and Pavana, the god of wind.

A large shalmali tree was found growing on the top of the Himavat mountains. It was a centuries-old tree with widespread branches, a huge trunk and innumerable leaves. The tree had plenty of flowers and fruits and provided shelter to many parrots. Travellers from far-off places, caravans of merchants, ascetics, pilgrims, elephants and many other creatures used to rest for a while under this tree. One day, Sage Narada saw the tree providing a home to different birds and animals with its widespread and intact branches and attributed its actions to the friendship and goodness of Pavana, the god of wind. Pavana, with his great speed and force, can uproot the tallest and strongest tree from its site. But, on seeing the healthy shalmali tree without any disturbance, Narada emphasized the goodness of Pavana and the friendliness he showed to the tree through his continued protection.

Shalmali did not like Narada praising Pavana and told him that Pavana was neither a friend nor a well-wisher. The tree reiterated that she protected herself with fierce energy and might, and she was not afraid of the Wind God even when he was unleashing his wrath. An infuriated Narada admonished the tree and said that when Indra, Yama or Vaisravana (the lord of water) were not equal to Pavana, Shalmali was nothing in front of the Wind God. When many other trees, stronger than Shalmali, bowed down their heads in respect to that deity, the arrogant talk of the tree showed only its folly.

Later, Narada relayed the tree's arrogance to the Wind God. Pavana, angered by this, approached Shalmali and told her that he had shown her mercy because Brahma, the Creator, had taken shelter under the tree once. Since the tree did not budge, Pavana wanted to test her power and might.

The night descended and Shalmali was left alone; She thought over the issue and finally came to a conclusion. The tree understood that the wind with great fury could easily injure her and it was not wise to compete with Pavana. So, with great sorrow, she self-pruned the branches and discarded her foliage and flowers. The next morning, when the Wind God came raging to tear the tree down, the tree was in a forlorn condition. On seeing the tree in a pathetic state, the Wind God felt mercy towards Shalmali. Bhishma narrated the story to Yudhishthira and said that just as Shalmali felt ashamed by Pavana's words, a weak and foolish person must repent like Shalmali to avoid the enmity of a powerful foe.

Why Does the Shalmali Have Thorns? There is a story in the Mahabharata describing why the tree has thorns on its branches. As we know, Draupadi was the common wife of the five Pandava brothers. She had to be equally shared among all of them, and she had vowed not to display favouritism. There was a customary practice that she had to massage her husband's feet daily. Bhima was jealous of the other four and did not want her to massage them. So, he decided to play a trick on Draupadi. Once, during his turn, he put a log of shalmali in his bed and covered it with a bedsheet. The shalmali tree had smooth branches at that time with no thorns. Draupadi started massaging the log of wood without removing the bed cover, thinking that it was Bhishma. As she massaged, she became suspicious of the inertness of the body on the bed, and removed the bedsheet to find that she had been massaging a log of wood. All the while, Bhima was hiding in the room. He burst

A universe unto itself
Stunning image of the red silk-cotton tree flower shot by Shiv's fotografia,
https://tinyurl.com/4zu5y6we, licensed under CC BY-SA 4.0

out laughing on seeing her consternation. Feeling insulted and annoyed, Draupadi cursed the wood to have thorns on it so as to avoid any other woman facing such an awkward situation. Draupadi's curse was realized. When Bhima planted the log in the garden, it started growing thorns on its branches. That is said to be the origin of thorns on the tree branches.

According to the Vishnu Purana, the principal tree of Kali Yuga is shalmali. It says that Earth is divided into seven concentric islands (*saptadweepa*) separated by seven seas. The islands or *dweepa*s are named after trees with one exception, which is named after a bird. At the core of the concentric islands is Jambudweepa (on which India is located), which is named after the Indian blackberry or jamun (*Syzygium cumini*). The third island, Shalmalidweepa, is named after the shalmali tree (*Shalmalia malabarica*).

Shalmali is also mentioned as 'semal' in Guru Granth Sahib, the holy book of the Sikhs, with the following commentary: 'The semal tree is tall and stiff as an arrow, but birds that visit it hopefully depart disappointed. For its fruits are tasteless and flowers nauseating. Only humility and sweetness, O Nanak, bear virtue and goodness.'*

The shalmali tree is considered inauspicious in the Dungarpur district of Rajasthan due to the hooting of owls that make the tree their home.

Another interesting story related to shalmali and about the tradition of Holi is narrated in the Bhagavata Purana. Hiranyakashipu, the demon king, after obtaining a boon, believed that he was no less than God and forced everyone to worship him. But his son Prahalad refused to obey. The demon king subjected Prahalad to gruesome punishments. Meanwhile, the child remained engrossed in worshipping Lord Vishnu. An enraged Hiranyakashipu sought the help of his sister Holika to get rid of Prahalad. She had a magical cloak that protected her from being harmed by fire. So, in order to get rid of Prahalad, she tricked him into sitting on her lap in a bonfire. When the flames engulfed them, the

---

*'Silk-Cotton Tree Benefits', *Astromantra*, https://tinyurl.com/bde2pcv6. Accessed on 2 August 2023.

cloak flew off Holika and enveloped Prahalad instead. Thus, Holika was burnt to death and Prahalad escaped unharmed. In North India, when the burning of Holika is symbolically re-enacted on the eve of the Holi festival, the demoness Holika is represented by a pole, usually of the shalmali tree, which is then set on fire to celebrate the victory of good over evil.

Shalmali, the God Tree: Since the Vedic period, this tree has been considered as a god tree. This is said to be the star tree of people born in Jyestha constellation, and it is strongly believed that planting of this tree and nurturing it may bring good luck to them. The Godhood concept attached to the tree has developed different ways for ethno-conservation. As the tree is believed to be the home of female tree spirits called yakshis, it is worshipped by women for the gift of children, leading to its conservation.

Traditions and Ethno-Conservation

Many folktales, songs, customs and traditions have been developed in association with this tree by different tribes in India. The Bhil tribe in Rajasthan worship and conserve the tree as it is considered a tree totem. The Garasia tribe of Rajasthan protects the tree in a sacred grove known as Maad Bavasi and treats it as one of its own. In a song sung by them in praise of the tree, the moon and clouds are declared as the tree's father and mother, respectively, and the village chief and his wife are assigned the role of its brother and sister-in-law, respectively. A humble request is made then to plant the tree and nurture it carefully. The Khuman clan of the Meitei community in Manipur never uses the tree in any form and protects it through environmental ethics. The tribal communities of Madhya Pradesh and Chhattisgarh also follow different methods for conserving the tree by following various ethno-conservation measures.

The red silk-cotton tree is a multipurpose tree species providing food, fodder, fibre, fuel and medicine, besides many ecological benefits. A study undertaken in southern Rajasthan on this tree has justified that this species is an 'Umbrella Tree Species' or life support tree for many animal species of forests of that region.[*] About 43 animal species have been observed visiting this tree for food, shelter or roosting. Out of these, 29 species were of avian fauna, 11 species were mammals, two species were arthropods and one was a reptile. As this drought-tolerant and easily propagable tree species plays an important role in balancing the forest ecosystem, it should be planted and protected as a keystone resource for many animal species. This lofty tree species is also designated as the king of the forest.

Usage

The dry cores of the *Salmalia malabarica* flower are an important ingredient for the spicy noodle soup in northern

*Jain, V. 'Bombax ceiba Linn.: As an Umbrella Tree Species in Forests of Southern Rajasthan, India', *Research Journal of Environmental Sciences*, Vol. 5. No. 8, p. 722–729, https://tinyurl.com/vp3vrru9. Accessed on 2 August 2023.

Thai cuisine. The silk-cotton is used for stuffing pillows, but is inferior to that of *Ceiba pentandra* (white silk-cotton). Its wood is used for creating packing cases, tea chests, boats, matches, etc.

The flowers are also used for treating piles, haemorrhoids and skin troubles. Mature fruits are used in the treatment of ulceration of kidney and bladder, chronic inflammation and calculi-related disorders. A paste made of thorns is used to treat pimples and acne. The bark is used to stop bleeding and treat wounds. Seeds are used to cure chronic cystitis and gonorrhoea. The gum of this tree is used to treat burning sensation, dysentery, influenza, pulmonary tuberculosis and enteritis. Roots are used to treat dysentery, diarrhoea and wounds.

Cultivation Practices

The red silk-cotton tree can be raised either by direct sowing or planting nursery raised seedlings. Two or three seeds are sown 15 cm apart in May–June in containers. Germination takes place from a few days to about four weeks. The germination percentage of fresh seeds is 50 per cent or less. Six-month-old seedlings can be planted at a wide spacing of 5 m × 5 m as this species has a very wide spreading crown. Stumps prepared from one-year-old nursery saplings are recommended for planting.

Flame of the Forest

Flame of the Forest (*Butea monosperma*)

Flame of the Forest

Family: Fabaceae

The flame of the forest, scientifically known as *Butea monosperma* (Lam.) Taub, belongs to the Fabaceae family. While the name 'Butea' was given in honour of a patron of botany, John Stuart (1713–1792), the Earl of Bute, 'monosperma' means one seed. Another name of the tree is *Butea frondosa* where 'frondosa' means leafy. In Sanskrit, it is known as *palash*, which means both leafy and beautiful. This name is derived from the town of Palashi, popular for the historic Battle of Plassey fought there. Palash is the state flower of Jharkhand.

The flame of the forest is a slow-growing, moderate-sized deciduous tree with crooked and irregular bole, growing to a height of 15 m. The tree is drought-resistant and frost-hardy. The leaves are alternate and trifoliate. The flowers are showy with a bright orange-red colour. The tree flowers in February–March and fruits in June–July.

Apart from flame of the forest, it is also known as bastard teak. The tree is called *polash* in Assamese; *kino* and palash in Bengali; *dhak*, palash, and *tesu* in Hindi; *muthuga* in Kannada; *plaasi, brahmavriksham, pu-palasu* and *chamata* in Malayalam; *pangong* in Manipuri; *palas, paras* and *kakracha* in Marathi; *kimsuka* in Sanskrit; and *elaiporasu, porasu* and *palasu* in Tamil. Some other names are *palasa* and *raktapushpa*.

Habitat and Distribution

This tree grows in drier areas in tropical and subtropical climates at elevations up to 1,500 m. While it grows best in alluvial soil, this tree can be grown in a wide variety of soils including shallow, gravelly sites, black cotton soil, clay loams and saline and waterlogged soils; it even responds well to coppicing. This tree is native to tropical and subtropical parts of the Indian subcontinent and Southeast Asia, across India, Bangladesh, Nepal, Sri Lanka, Myanmar, Thailand, Laos, Cambodia, Vietnam, Malaysia and western Indonesia. This tree has successfully been acclimatized in Israel as an exotic species. It has also been introduced in Zimbabwe.

Palash–Flame of the Forest: When the trees are in full bloom with bright orange flowers, they glow like a flame in the midst of the forest, leading to its name. This tree is associated with spring in West Bengal, especially through the poems and songs of Nobel Laureate Rabindranath Tagore, who compared its bright orange flowers to fire. In Jharkhand, this tree is associated with folk traditions. Many folk tales describe palash as a forest fire. During February-March, when most trees have shed their leaves, palash is in full bloom.

Religious Significance

In Indian mythology, palash is associated with Pooram, one of the stars in the almanac. In Telangana, the flowers of this tree are used to worship Lord Shiva on the occasion of Shivaratri and are called *modugu chettu* in Telugu. Small chips of palash wood are used for *agnihotra* or the fire ritual. This tree can be found in most of the old Kerala Brahmin houses as it is mainly used for their agnihotra. It is a main component in the agnihotra rituals of Tamil Brahmins, especially during the first year of *brahmacharya* performed for *brahmachari*s. In Theravada Buddhism, this tree is said to have been used for attaining enlightenment by the Buddha. In Punjabi literature, palash has been praised extensively. The Punjabi poet Harinder Singh Mehboob has employed it as a symbol in his poems. There is also a mention of this tree in the first shloka of the Shukla Yajur Veda. The palash flower is also used to symbolize the arrival of spring and the colour of love in Sanskrit. In the Gita Govindam, Jayadeva compares this flower to the red nails of Kamadeva, with which he wounds the hearts of lovers. There is a strong belief that one who plants and nurtures this tree will ultimately attain the world of Lord Brahma and, consequently, of salvation.

The palash tree is worshipped in about 11 temples of Lord Vishnu and Lord Shiva. Ten villages have been named after this tree in Tamil Nadu. About 77 villages in states like Andhra Pradesh, Assam, Chhattisgarh, Gujarat, Madhya Pradesh, Maharashtra, Odisha, Punjab, Rajasthan, Uttar Pradesh and West Bengal have been named after this tree. The tree is also discussed by the famous Tamil saint-poet Thirugnanasambandar in Thevaram.

Mythological Significance

This tree is sacred to both Hindus and Buddhists. It is considered sacred by Hindus because of the trifoliate formation of its leaves, which represents the Trimurti. The tree is linked to the moon as it is believed to have originated from a falcon's feather infused with soma, the gods' intoxicating drink, granting it immortality and significance. Dry twigs of the tree are used in the sacred fire while performing *homam* or *havan*, a sacred fire ritual. Its wood is considered sacrificial as mentioned in the Vedas. Utensils made by using palasha wood are used for sacred rituals. The stick that Brahmin boys use during the sacred thread ceremony is also made from the wood of this tree. When a Brahmin boy becomes a *sadhu* after renouncing worldly life, and his hair is shorn, he is given the leaves of this tree to eat.

The orange-red flowers are dedicated to the gods, particularly to Goddess Kali. During the spring festival of Holi, a dye obtained from the flowers is used to sprinkle on passers-by. As Holi is associated with Lord Krishna, the tree has also been associated with him. Palash wood is used in ceremonies connected with Krishnashtami Vratham and the digging of tanks.

According to Puranic legends, the palash tree has an association with Brahma as well. Once, when Shiva and Parvathi were engaged in the amorous act, Agni, in the guise of a Brahmin, spied on them on the orders of other gods and deities, including Brahma. Enraged by this, Parvathi cursed the whole host of those gods and deities to be born as trees. Because of the curse, Brahma became palash, Vishnu became *aswatha* or peepal and Rudra into the *vata* or banyan.

When in bloom, the tree, from a distance, gives the appearance of a fire on the horizon. In *Ritusamhara*, Kalidasa describes the jungles of palash trees as resembling a blazing fire, making the Earth look like a newly-wed bride with red garments. The poet Amir Khusrau compared the palash flowers with lion's blood-stained claws.

According to a Hindu superstition, if the root of a palash tree is gathered when the Ashvini constellation rules the season (mid-September to mid-October) and is tied to a man's arm, he will be able to make any woman to fall in love with him by touching her.

The curious formation of its flowers is the subject of many riddles in Bihar. One of them is:

An Elephant Tusk;
But not a Tusk!
The Body of a Monk;
But not a Monk!
The Head of a Crow;
But not a Crow!
But a Parakeet!

Here, the dark glossy black calyx is the head of the crow. The petals are the colour of a monk's robe. The prominent stamen is the tusk. And the keel is the beak of the parakeet.

Though the flowers are beautiful, they do not have any fragrance. In ancient books, a person with beauty but lacking moral or intellectual qualities is termed as a human palash.

How Did the Soma Leaf Grow into Palash on Earth? An early Indo-Aryan tale narrates how the palash tree came to be. One day, Indra, the chief of the gods, was feeling extremely thirsty. The other gods requested Goddess Gayatri to go over to the celestial mountain Mujavana where the soma creeper

Flame of the Forest
Butea monosperma clicked at Morni Hills (Panchkula) by Varinder Naturaphile,
https://tinyurl.com/47cp7sbh, licensed under CC BY-SA 4.0

grew and bring it back, so that Indra would have uninterrupted supply of soma forever. Gayatri, in the form of an eagle, flew to the mountain, swooped down and seized the creeper in her beak in the midst of tight security. Before the guards could do anything, she flew away. But, somehow, an arrow shot by one of the guards, Krishanu, missed Gayatri and struck the vine. One of the leaves fell on Earth and grew into the palash tree. This is how the palash tree grew from the soma leaf.

Devotees of Lord Shiva and Lord Vishnu paint their foreheads with a deep orange-red dye obtained from the flowers of the tree. In the Mahabharata, the Sage Jamadagni conducted a gods' sacrifice in Palasvana, the palash tree grove, attended by all the rivers.

There is an intriguing Koraput tribal legend of Odisha about the first palash tree. Long ago, the tribes of Pengu, Muria and Bhattra were led by Chaitu Bhattra, whose daughter was unwillingly married and later fell in love with another dark, handsome Muria man, with whom she had secret rendezvous. When her husband was informed by the villagers, he set a trap for his wife. One day, he told his wife that he would return in a few days after visiting his sister's house in the next village. He tied his clothes together and set out with his staff. He actually went up to the forest and, after spending some time there, returned home late at night. On seeing the Muria boy in his hut, he became very angry and beat them with his stick, eventually killing them both. Then he threw their corpses into the forest. Both bodies bled, and their blood reached a stream. A tree with red flowers grew from this stream, and this is believed to be the first palash tree that appeared on Earth according to the tribes of Koraput.

The Buddhists associate the tree in flower to penitents dressed in orange-red, worn symbolically by those who have renounced all their desires. The tree also finds a place in Buddhist *jataka* stories.

Usage

The leaves are stitched together to make biodegradable plates. This tree acts as a windbreak and plays a key role in fixing nitrogen in the soil. As the wood is durable under water, it is used for well curbs, piles and water scoops. Spoons and ladles made of the palash wood are used in Hindu rituals to pour ghee into the fire. The tree is considered the best for lac production after the kusum tree (*Schleichera oleosa*). The flowers yield yellow dye and a decoction made from them is used to keep white ants out of fields. The bark is used for tanning. The gum obtained from the tree, known as Bengal kino, is highly valued by druggists due to its astringent properties, and by leather workers because of its rich tannin content. The gum is also used in certain food dishes. The dye obtained from the flowers is used as a fabric dye.

Apart from trade usage, the leaves, too, have medicinal use. The leaf juice is used to treat boils, pimples, tumours, worm infestations and haemorrhoids. The flowers are used to treat leprosy, skin diseases, asthma, sunstroke, diarrhoea and eye diseases. The gum is applied externally to treat ulcers. It is given orally to treat diarrhoea and dysentery. The red juice gum is applied to bruises and inflammations. The Bengal kino is used to treat diabetes, leprosy, skin diseases and fever. The bark is used to treat liver disorders, dysmenorrhoea and gonorrhoea. The root bark is used to treat haemorrhoids, ulcers, tumours and dropsy. Palash seeds are used for treating roundworms, skin diseases, tumours, piles and eye diseases.

Cultivation Practices

Mature pods are collected and dried in the hot sun. The seeds are then separated by beating the pods. About 1,480 seeds can be contained in 1 kg of pods. The seeds can be stored in airtight containers for one year and can be sown with a spacing of 3 m × 3 m. Germination starts within 10–12 days. The tree may attain a height of 4 m within three years. Plantations can be established in irrigated as well as rain-fed land.

Alexandrian Laurel (*Calophyllum inophyllum*)

Alexandrian Laurel

Family: Calophyllaceae

The Alexandrian laurel, scientifically known as *Calophyllum inophyllum* L., belongs to the Calophyllaceae family. '*Calophyllum*' means beautiful leaf; '*inophyllum*' means leaf with conspicuous venation. Both the names describe the characters of the leaf. The species that grows in the Western Ghats is called *Calophyllum elatum* Bedd., and the species that grows on riverbanks and backwaters of the Indian west coast is named *Calophyllum apetalum* Willd. C.

The tree is a slow-growing and medium-sized evergreen tree with a spreading crown. This generally grows up to 25 m. The trunk is usually short and twisted. The oblong/oval leaves with acute base are smooth and shining. The tree flowers in March–April. The fragrant flowers are white in colour. Fruiting occurs in May–June. The globose drupes are smooth and green.

While the trade and the common English name is Alexandrian laurel, it is also called *tamanu*, Indian laurel, mastwood, beach calophyllum, oil-nut tree and beauty leaf. This is known as *sultan champa* in Hindi; *surahonne* and *honne kaayi mara* in Kannada; *surampunna*, *punna* and *pinna* in Malayalam; *surangi* in Marathi; *punnaga*, *nagchampa* and *panch kasara* in Sanskrit; *punnai* and *pinnai* in Tamil; *puna* and *poona* in Telugu; and *surangi* and *undi* in Urdu.

Habitat and Distribution

This tree grows just above the high-tide mark on rocky and sandy shores. This can also be found on islands and inland areas, particulary on sandy soils at elevations up to 200 meters. This tree is found along the coastal areas of the Indian and Pacific oceans from East Africa through Asia to Australia and the Pacific Islands. Now, this species is widely cultivated in all the tropical regions of the world. This is best known as an ornamental tree because of its decorative leaves, fragrant flowers and spreading crown.

Religious Significance

While performing religious rites on Ganesh Chaturthi, Hindus offer 21 types of flowers, leaves, grasses, fruits and grains. Punnaga, the Sanskrit name of the tree, is one of those 21 types of flowers.

This flower is sacred to Lord Vishnu and is offered while worshipping him. It is also used as a garland for decorating his neck. As a fragrant flower, it adorns the hair of Goddess Lalithambika in the Lalitha Sahasranamam. In Carnatic music, there are many interesting references to the punnaga flower—a flower for worship and adornment for different gods. It is believed that the famous raga Punnaagavaraali is named after this tree. The leaves or flowers of this tree are offered to Lord Vishnu on Narasimha Jayanthi Vrata and Goddess Saraswati on Shree Saraswati Vrata.

∾

Punnaga, One of Shiva's Favourite Trees: It is said that Mylapore was once known as Punnaivanam. Lord Shiva at the Kapaleeswarar temple in Mylapore, Chennai is also known as 'Punnaivananathar' (Lord of Punnai Grove). It is believed that the punnaga tree, the sthalavriksham, is as old as the temple, which was built in the sixteenth century by the Vijayanagar kings. The presiding goddess is known as Karpagambal, and the name translates to goddess of the wish-yielding tree. Tamil literature has classified punnaga as a tree suitable for a neithal landscape (coastal region or sea shore; as per classical Tamil Sangam literature).

The Nithyakalyana Perumal temple is located in Thiruvidanthai, with a magnificent punnai tree along the East Coast Road of Chennai. The Archaeological Survey of India (ASI), which maintains the temple, has erected an information board displaying the age of the temple as 1,000 years. The temple's pillars have carvings of Lord Krishna dancing on the punnaga tree.

More than 30 temples in Tamil Nadu consider punnaga to be sacred. Lord Shiva, named Punnaivana Nathar after this tree, is worshipped in Mylapore and Tiruppurambayam in Tamil Nadu. More than 40 villages have been named after this tree. In states like Andhra Pradesh and Kerala, about 20 villages have been named after this tree. Interesting proverbs have been developed by using the name of this tree as well. This tree has about 50 special names in Tamil. Famous Tamil Poets like Kambar, Kalladar, Ilangovadikal, Thirugnanasambandar, Thirumoolar, Pugazhenthi, Nakkeerar, Naladiyar, etc., have given unique names to this tree in Tamil literature. Men are commonly named after this tree.

Uses

The pulp of immature fruits is reported as edible. The oil obtained from the seeds is used in lamps. The oil can be used in soap production, as skin moisturizer and as hair oil after refining. The oil that is extracted by crushing the fruits is used to scent coconut oil and also used as hair oil. The stones of the fruits are used as marbles. The sticky latex is used to caulk canoes. The mature fruit is burned as a mosquito repellent. The punnaga wood is used in the construction of canoes and small boats, masts, keels, pulley blocks, construction, carpentry, flooring, stairs, furniture, cabinet work, cart-wheel hubs, vessels and musical instruments. The tree is often planted along roadsides for shade and in gardens as ornamental trees as well as along hedges as a windbreak. One of the most important uses of this tree is in reforestation schemes.

Punnaga is commonly used in traditional medicine. The seed oil is used to treat a wide range of skin problems. A root decoction is used to treat ulcers, boils and ophthalmia. The latex is used to treat rheumatism and psoriasis. The latex and pounded bark are applied on wounds and ulcers and also used to treat orchitis and lung affections. This is also used to treat gonorrhoea, as a purgative and after childbirth. The punnaga resin is used to treat wounds and insect bites. A leaf infusion is used to treat sore eyes, haemorrhoids and dysentery. Boiled leaves are applied as poultice to cuts, sores, ulcers, boils and skin rash. The seed oil is used externally to treat swellings, ulcers, scabies, ringworm, boils and itch. The flowers are used to prepare heart tonics.

Flowers of *Calophyllum inophyllum* in Visakhapatnam
Shot by Adityamadhav83, https://tinyurl.com/2p853798, licensed under CC BY-SA 3.0

Economic Significance

This species is most suitable for growing along the seashore. It can also be grown in areas where other trees cannot grow. It can be grown in coastal villages on a large scale. Fisherwomen can be involved in collection of the fruits, enabling additional income. The seeds collected can be used for manufacturing soap. The trees, growing against the windward direction along the coast, act as a windbreak. They prevent deposit of sand due to heavy wind and storm. They also filter the salt deposit of the seaborne wind to a great extent. As a result, the yield of agricultural crops may be increased considerably. As the tree is drought tolerant, it can be planted all along the coast of India. In towns and cities, this tree can be planted for ornamental purposes in the premises of big buildings. *Calophyllum elatum* and *Calophyllum apetalum* also can be used for this purpose. They are known for purifying the atmospheric air as well.

Cultivation Practices

The seeds are collected by cutting open the pericarp of mature fruits. The seeds are to be dibbled in the nursery bed. Fresh nuts may germinate after 60 days. Up to 95 per cent germination is expected. Seedlings that are 30 days old can be transplanted into containers. One-year-old seedlings after hardening for three months can be planted. Planting can be done at an espacement of 4 m × 4 m. Watering is necessary for two years till the plants get established. This is one of the important tree-borne oilseed species. A five-year-old tree may yield 12 kg of fruits. Fruiting commences at four to five years.

Coconut Palm (*Cocos nucifera*)

Coconut Palm

Family: Arecaceae

Coconut palm, scientifically known as *Cocos nucifera* Linn., belongs to the Arecaceae family. In Portuguese, '*Cocos*' means grimace because the fruit is believed to resemble a monkey's head, with the three holes at the nut's base giving it a grinning face appearance. '*Nucifera*' is Latin for nut bearing. The Sanskrit word '*narikela*' is derived from the term '*narik*', which means 'with water'.

The coconut palm is the only species in the genus *Cocos*. This is a tall palm that usually grows to a height of 30 m, with a smooth trunk. Flowering and fruiting occur throughout the year, but mainly in dry weather. It is said to be mostly cross-pollinated, though some dwarf varieties are self-pollinating.

The trade name of this tree is coconut palm. It is called *dab* and *narkol* in Bengali; *nariyal* and *khopra* in Hindi; *thengina* in Kannada; *narlu* in Konkani; *thengu*, *thenna* and *tenga* in Malayalam; *yubi* in Manipuri; *naral* and *shripal* in Marathi; *narikela*, *narikera* and *suphala* in Sanskrit; *thennai* in Tamil; and *tenkaya*, *narikelamu* and *tenkai* in Telugu.

Habitat and Distribution

This tree is commonly found along tropical coasts, sometimes extending inland on alluvial plains and avoiding waterlogged soils. Coconut grows well in lowland tropical regions and up to a maximum elevation of about 1,000 m. This tree grows best in areas with high rainfall.

The origin of this tree is a subject of controversy. While some authorities claim that this is native to Southeast Asia, others claim that its origin lies in the northwest of South America. Fossil records from New Zealand indicate that small, coconut-like trees had grown there about fifteen million years ago. It is said that even older fossils have been identified in Rajasthan and Maharashtra in India. This is grown in countries like Indonesia, the Philippines, India, the Maldives, Middle East, United States of America, Australia and Bermuda.

Religious Significance

Coconut plays an important role in Hindu rituals. Coconut is invariably offered while worshipping a Hindu god or goddess. In Maharashtra, during the celebration of Narali Purnima, a full moon that occurs at the end of the monsoon season, coconut is offered for worship. Irrespective of their religion, the fishermen offer coconut to the rivers and the sea while celebrating the beginning of a new fishing season in the hope of getting a good catch. Hindus break a coconut when initiating a new activity or undertaking a new enterprise, hoping to get the blessings of the god or goddess for successful completion of the activity.

∽

Coconut-Breaking Ritual for Fulfilment of the Wishes: The Hindu goddess of wealth, Lakshmi, is often depicted as holding a coconut in her hand. At the base of the Rock Fort temple in Tiruchirappalli, coconuts are broken daily by devotees in a place marked for this purpose in the shrine of God Manikka

Vinayagar. Some devotees break 108 coconuts when their wish is fulfilled. This kind of offering of coconuts takes place in almost all the Hindu temples as per the prayer. Generally, it is considered auspicious to break a coconut as a part of religious and cultural rituals.

In Hindu marriages, coconuts are placed on a silver plate as it is considered a symbol of auspiciousness. Both Hindus and Buddhists display coconut flowers and tender fruits as a symbol of sacredness during wedding ceremonies and other important rituals. In Kerala, coconut flowers are inserted into brass vessels filled with paddy and exhibited in prominent places during wedding ceremonies. The same is also followed in Sri Lanka. Spotting a coconut the moment one wakes up on the Hindu New Year is regarded as an auspicious sign. In West Bengal, people believe that as the coconut has eyes, it will never fall on a passer-by. In certain communities of southern India, cut coconut is thrown over the heads of bridegrooms to scare away evil spirits. Goddess Bhadrakalai is offered a coconut in place of human sacrifice as the coconut resembles a human head. In Western India, coconuts are thrown into the sea at the end of the monsoons to appease the waters. The tree is treated as a family god in Gujarat.

In the Philippines, a community fills two halved coconut shells with sweet cooked rice and places a halved boiled egg on top. This is offered to the deceased and ancestors along with prayers during a ritual known as Niniyogan.

The coconut palm is worshipped as a sacred tree in about five temples in Tamil Nadu. In Aduthurai of Thanjavur district in Tamil Nadu, Lord Shiva is called Kulaivanangeesar after this

Close-up of a coconut inflorescence

tree. More than 30 villages in Tamil Nadu have been named after this tree. Dozens of puzzles and proverbs have been developed using the name of this tree. Famous Tamil poets like Kambar, Nakkeerar, Ilangovadikal, Uruththirankannanaar, Seeththalaisaaththanaar, Vallalaar, etc., have described the coconut palm with special names. Both men and women are commonly named after this tree in Tamil Nadu. In Thevaram, the young saint–poet Thirugnanasambandar has composed poems praising this tree.

Mythological Significance

A folktale from Kerala narrates how the coconut got its face. Once, there was a young fisherman from Kerala who did not know how to catch fish. Even though he tried with nets and poles, he could not get any fish. Others laughed at his poor condition. Therefore, he planned to learn some magic. He visited a magician and learnt how to remove the head from the body from him. During the evening, when all fishermen returned to their hamlets and there was no one around, he would go to the beach, remove his head from his body at an isolated spot and dive into the water. On seeing a strange figure, the fishes would cluster around and the small fishes would enter his body through his neck. The man would swim back to the shore, take the fishes out and replace his head. After reaching the village, he would show the villagers all the fish he had caught. The man never revealed the secret to anyone. The fishermen became curious as this man was getting good catch without a pole or net. One day, a small boy followed him. The boy saw him take off his head and dive into the sea. The little boy snatched the head and carried it for some distance. As the head was too heavy, the boy threw it into a nearby bush. After some time, when the man came out of the water, he could not see his head. He searched for his head and realized that his magic was running out of time. As there was no other way, he jumped into the sea and became a fish. The small boy who reached the village brought all the villagers to the shore to show them the miraculous head. Upon reaching the bush located on the beach, they were astonished to discover that the once small head had transformed into a tall and graceful palm tree, adorned with nuts. Every nut bore the man's face on it. It is believed that the coconut was created thus!

How the Coconut Tree Came to Earth: In a Hindu mythological story, Trishanku, a famous king belonging to the Solar dynasty (also known as the Ikshvaku dynasty), was a pious person and was very devoted to the gods. He had one desire, and it was to go to heaven with his mortal body intact. He did not want to wait till he died. Sage Vishvamitra and his family lived in a forest of the kingdom. At that time, there was severe famine in the country. Since the sage had gone over to another country, his family was starving. Knowing this, King Trishanku helped the family with food and other requirements. On his return, the sage came to know about the help rendered by the king and promised to help the king to get his desire fulfilled. The sage started performing a yajna or sacrifice to the gods. When the fire and the prayers became strong, the king started rising off the ground, moved above the Earth and the clouds, and neared the gates of heaven where the gods lived. Seeing the mortal body of a human intact at the gates, the gods rushed to their king, Indra, and complained. Sighting the body of King Trishanku near the gate, Indra became angry and pushed the king down. While falling, Trishanku cried out of fear. Hearing the desperate call of the king, the sage looked up and ordered him to stay where he was. King Trishanku stopped mid-air. Sage Vishvamitra knew that the king could stay there only for a while as his power was wearing off. So, the sage held the king up with a long pole. In time, this pole created by the sage became the trunk of the coconut tree and Trishanku's head became the coconut fruit.

Uses

The leaves of the coconut palm are interwoven and used as thatching material for huts. They can be woven into mats, baskets, etc. The midribs of the leaflets are used for brooms. The fibre obtained can be used for mats, brush, ropes and for stuffing mattresses and upholstery. Its fruits or seeds are a versatile food. They are eaten raw and used in a wide range of cooked dishes as well. The dried fruit is shredded and used in cakes, curries, etc. Coconut milk or cream obtained from the fruit is an important ingredient in many African and Asian cuisines and bakery products. The gelatinous flesh inside a half-ripe seed is relished as a delicacy and is often consumed raw. The edible oil obtained from the seeds is used in cooking, ice cream, confectioneries, soaps, detergents, cosmetics, candles, pharmaceuticals, etc. The liquid inside unripe fruits is a deliciously refreshing drink. A sugary sap obtained by cutting the stalk of the inflorescence is fermented into an alcoholic drink. The hard and woody shell surrounding the seed is used to make cups, bowls, buttons, combs, bangles, musical instruments, etc. The wood is used for rafters, spear handles, walking sticks, picture frames, poles, etc.

The seed oil is rubbed on the joints to relieve pain. This is used to treat rheumatism and back pain and also to maintain smooth and soft skin. The oil is mixed with turmeric and used to treat sick new-borns and women who have just given birth. It is also used to treat fish poisoning. The juice from green coconut is given to women who have difficult pregnancies. The juice of the fruit is used to treat kidney problems. In the Solomon Islands, parts of the tree are used to treat diarrhoea and dysentery.

Cultivation Practices

Nuts are collected from selected mother trees for seed propagation. For producing a large number of progenies, tissue culture is a popular method of vegetative propagation. The tall varieties reproduce by cross-pollination. The dwarf varieties reproduce through self-pollination. The tall palms mature slowly and flower in 6–10 years with a life span of 80–100 years. The dwarf palms bear flowers in three to four years with a life span of 30–40 years. The coconut trees flower and fruit throughout the year.

Banyan Tree (*Ficus benghalensis*)

Banyan

Family: Moraceae

The banyan tree, scientifically known as *Ficus benghalensis* L., belongs to the Moraceae family. This is known as the banyan, banyan fig or Indian banyan and is the national tree of India. The largest trees of this species, with wide canopy coverage, are found only in India. It is said that the British had given the name banyan to this tree as banias or Hindu merchants assembled under this tree for business and worship. '*Ficus*' means fig and '*benghalensis*' pertains to Bengal. The Sanskrit name for this tree, *vata*, means to surround or encompass.

This is a large, evergreen tree, epiphytic in its early stage, with numerous aerial roots up to 15 m on its branches. The long and descending aerial roots that grow as woody stems ultimately become stilts. Banyan is planted mostly along avenues for shade. The fig is scarlet red when ripe. Wasps and birds play a major role in pollination and reproduction of this species.

As mentioned before, the trade name of this tree is banyan. The English names are banyan tree, Indian banyan tree or East Indian fig tree. This is called *bot* and *bor-goch* in Assamese; bot in Bengali; *vad* in Gujarati; *bar* and *bargad* in Hindi; *alada* in Kannada; *per-al* and *al* in Malayalam; *vad* in Marathi; vata in Sanskrit; *ala*, *al* and *per-al* in Tamil; and *mari* and *pedda-mari* in Telugu.

Habitat and Distribution

This is found growing in all places from sea level up to 1,200 m in deciduous and semi-evergreen forests. This is drought resistant and can withstand mild frost. This is considered native to tropical Asia, from India to Myanmar, Thailand, southern China and Malaysia. This has also been cultivated and naturalized in many tropical regions of the world including western Africa, North America, the West Indies, Australia, the Middle East and many islands in the Pacific Ocean.

Religious Significance

The banyan, along with the Ganges and the Himalayas, symbolize India. The tree is rarely disturbed, except on the very rare occasion of collecting its leaves during famine as fodder for the cattle. The Trimurti, namely Vishnu, Brahma and Shiva, are symbolized by its bark, roots and branches, respectively. Kubera, the treasure keeper of the gods, is also known as Vatashraya, which means one who lives in the banyan tree. According to a Puranic legend, this tree is visited by Goddess Lakshmi on Sundays.

Another tale talks about Savitri, who lost her husband under a banyan tree one year after her marriage. It is said that she succeeded in bringing her husband to life again by worshipping the tree. As the legend has become very popular, women fast and worship the tree as a part of a special pooja on Vat Savitri day by circumambulating the tree for long and healthy lives of their husbands. On this day, married Hindu women tie threads around the tree and pray to the tree for divine grace to secure the lives of their husbands and to get the same husband in the subsequent births as well.

An anecdote in the Mahabharata mentions that a woman and her daughter who worshipped the banyan tree and embraced it became the mothers of Sage Vishvamitra and Sage Jamadagni. Traditionally, those who want to have children circumambulate the tree on auspicious days and worship it as it is regarded as a symbol of fertility.

In the Hattipala Jataka, the story states that a woman was blessed with seven sons by praying to the deity of the banyan tree. It is said that if one undertakes a pilgrimage to one of the main banyan trees, it is considered equivalent to 12 years of sacrifice. It is believed that if one anoints oneself with the ashes of any part of the banyan tree, they become free of all sins.

∼

Banyan, a Star Tree: In Hindu mythology, the banyan tree is associated with the star Makom. This is a robust and firm tree with milky latex and bound by adventitious roots. It cools the atmosphere by giving shade. People call this *vatah*. Other names include *rektaphala* (bearing reddish fruit), *sringi* (aerial roots), *nygrodha* (blocking the way due to adventitious roots), *skandhaja* (sprouting from the stem cuttings), *drumah* (firm tree), *kshiri* (indicating the presence of latex), *bahupaadah* (having many legs or adventitious roots supporting the branches) and *vaisravanavaso* (Bodhi tree of Sravana or Visravana). The bark of this tree is one of the ingredients of the popular Ayurvedic formulation Panchavalkala (bark of five trees). This combination is used for treating skin diseases due to pitta.

∼

There are about 30 temples in Tamil Nadu where the banyan tree is worshipped as a sacred tree. In about six temples of Lord Shiva, the god has been named after this tree. Nearly 192 villages have been named after this tree in Tamil Nadu. In states like Andhra Pradesh, Assam, Bihar, Gujarat, Himachal Pradesh, Karnataka, Kerala, Madhya Pradesh, Maharashtra, Nagaland, Odisha, Punjab, Rajasthan, Uttar Pradesh and West Bengal, about 200 villages have been named after this tree. Many proverbs and puzzles have been developed in Tamil. Both men and women are commonly named after this tree. In, Thevaram, Thirunavukkarasar has composed poems praising the banyan tree.

Mythological Significance

In Hindu mythology, it is said that Lord Vishnu was born under the shade of the banyan tree. The Kalpavriksha or the wish-granting tree, often depicted as a banyan tree, has a Buddhist sculpture in Besnagar, which is now exhibited in the Indian Museum, Kolkata. The tree was identified as the banyan tree by Ananda K. Coomaraswamy, an intellectual warrior, who waged a fierce war against attempts by missionaries and the West to distort and vilify Hinduism and its various facets.

In a traditional Aryan story, Indra is portrayed as sitting with his queen under the shade of a banyan tree from whose branches people collected jewels, clothes, food and drink. The banyan tree, also known as agastyavata, symbolizes immortality. During the great deluge, when the entire world was flooded, a leaf of the banyan tree cradled Balmukunda, the infant form of Lord Krishna, safely through the waters. In the Vishnu Purana, Vishnu is compared with the seed of the

Banyan fruits at Indira Gandhi Zoological Park, Visakhapatnam
Shot by Adityamadhav83, https://tinyurl.com/3zevwn3t, licensed under CC BY-SA 3.0

banyan. As a huge tree originates from a little seed, the entire universe is reduced to its germ after these periodic deluges. This germ is contained in Vishnu, who then recreates the universe.

According to a folktale of Ganjam district of Odisha, Nirantali, the first keeper of the world, was sent by the gods to live in Saphganna. She brought the banyan seed wrapped in leaves. Men came into being when the Earth and the clouds were ready. The banyan seeds were planted by them. The seeds grew into thin trees with tiny leaves providing no shade. Nirantali stretched the leaves till they became large and pulled the branches till they reached the Earth. Even then, men did not have proper food to eat. So, she ordered the banyan tree to feed the men with its milk. The tree replied that it had only blood and no milk. Nirantali hit the trunk of the tree with her axe and ordered it to produce milk. Men lived by drinking the milk until grain came into the world.

The Vishnu Purana states: 'As the wide-spreading Nargodha (Sanskrit name for Banyan) tree is compressed in a small seed, so at the time of dissolution, the whole universe is comprehended in Thee as its germ; as the Nargodha germinates from the seed, and becomes just a shoot and then rises into loftiness, the created world proceeds from Thee and expands into magnitude.'[*]

In Hinduism, the banyan leaf is said to be the resting place of Lord Krishna. In the Bhagavad Gita, Krishna says: 'There is a banyan tree which has its roots upward and its branches down, and the Vedic hymns are its leaves. One who knows this tree is the knower of the Vedas.'[**] He also says: 'Of all trees I am the banyan tree, and of the sages among the demigods I am Narada. Of the Gandharvas I am Citraratha, and among perfected beings I am the sage Kapila.'[***]

According to a Bhil legend from Rajasthan, the banyan tree is believed to have been originally situated in the garden of Vasuki, the great serpent lord of Patalaloka, the world of nether regions. Amba, the goddess of Earth, wanted to have it for her children. Since Vasuki was not ready to part with the tree, after a fight with Vasuki, with Lord Shiva's help, Amba managed to bring the banyan tree to the Earth.

The tree is considered sacred to the Buddhists. After

---

[*]The Saffron, 'Ancient India and its Relevance to Nature by Akshinta Das', https://tinyurl.com/yckrsp2w, Accessed on 2 August 2023.
[**]B.G. 15.1; 'Chapter 15: The Yoga of the Supreme Person', Bhagavad Gita, https://tinyurl.com/39395rar. Accessed on 2 August 2023
[***]B.G. 10.26

attaining enlightenment, the Buddha is said to have sat under a banyan tree for seven days and absorbed his newfound realization. The numerous branches of the banyan tree are believed to be the homes of gods and spirits. Lord Shiva is depicted as Dakshinamurthi sitting under a banyan tree with rishis at his feet.

The Great Banyan Tree of the Philippines: People in certain parts of the Philippines believe in sorcery, witchcraft and other supernatural powers. The villagers fear Baliti, the great banyan tree, which is believed to possess supernatural powers. It is believed that if anyone disrespects the tree, they will face its wrath. According to a legend, Baliti was a man possessed with great healing power. He was respected and loved by the people. Recognizing his good service to society, Goddess Engkantada granted him healing power beyond earthly means. Engkantada advised him to use the powers only to help others and not to take, demand or accept any payment in return for his healing, which Baliti agreed to. Baliti served the people for many years without taking any payment. After some time, he met a beautiful woman, Brunhilde, and married her. Brunhilde started demanding money for healing the sick. As the love between Baliti and Brunhilde became greater than his promise to Engkandata, he too demanded payment and accepted it for his service. His wife made the people fall sick using her sorceress powers. She would then tell the villagers that her husband alone could cure them. Thus, they lived lavishly. The poor villagers started hating Baliti and his wife and prayed to Goddess Engkandata. After confirming the wrongdoings of both Baliti and his wife, Goddess Engkandata turned Brunhilde into a snake and Baliti into a banyan tree, without taking away his powers as he was originally a good person. So, Baliti could still help the people who sought his aid. Many believe that Baliti's powers still exist. It is believed that if anybody offends the tree, tragedy occurs to the concerned. So, due respect and regard is given whenever people pass the tree.

Usage

The banyan leaf can be used as fodder. Leaves are stitched together to make biodegradable plates. The fruits are edible. The latex of all parts of the tree is used to produce inferior-quality rubber. The milky juice is converted into birdlime. The bark and leaves contain tannin. The aerial roots are commonly used as temporary binding material. The banyan wood is of poor quality and can be used as the linings of drawers and cabinets. It can also be used for poles, cart yokes, etc. This tree is often planted as an ornamental tree and for soil conservation. It is also cultivated as a shade tree along streets and in parks and gardens. It is grown as a host tree for lac insects as well. Many species of birds and bats visit the tree during the fruiting season.

The leaves are used for treating dysentery and diarrhoea. The young leaves are boiled and applied to abscesses to discharge pus. The concentrated latex combined with fruit is used to treat spermatorrhoea and gonorrhoea. The milky juice mixed with sugar is used to treat dysentery in children. The latex is applied to treat toothache, bruises, rheumatic joints and lumbago. The milky juice is dripped into wounds to kill germs. The bark is used as tonic and diuretic. The fruit is used as tonic as it has a cooling effect.

Landmark Trees

In certain places, the banyan tree becomes a landmark tree because of its size, age and extent of its coverage. The tree in Chicholi, Hoshangabad, spans an acre-and-a-half in width. The tree found in Chunchanakuppe, near Bengaluru, is said to be five centuries old spreading over three acres. The Great Banyan Tree found in the Acharya Jagadish Chandra Bose Botanical Garden near Kolkata, assessed to be about 250 years old, is declared as the widest tree in the world with 2,800 aerial roots and coverage of about 14,500 sq. m of land (3.5 acres). The canopy spread of the banyan tree located in Bithreddy village in Krishnagiri district of Tamil Nadu is around two acres.

Cultivation Practices

The banyan tree depends on a specific wasp species for pollination of its flowers, which set fruits and spread into new habitats. The tree can be raised through seeds that can be stored at room temperature for up to two years. It can also be propagated from cuttings or by transplanting young trees.

Aalada Marada Thimmakka: When one discusses the banyan tree, one cannot forget the great service of the 111-year-old Thimmakka of Karnataka state. Saalumarada Thimmakka, also known as Aalada Marada Thimmakka, is a popular Indian environmentalist. The Kannada word '*salumarada*' means row of trees; the words '*aalada marada*' mean the banyan tree. She has planted and nurtured over 400 banyan trees with the support of her husband along a 4-km stretch between Hulikal and Kudur in Karnataka. She has also raised 8,000 other trees. Though she has received many awards, her work was recognized by the Government of India recently and she was conferred with the Padma Shri award in 2019.

∾

Indian Fig Tree (*Ficus racemosa*)

Indian Fig

Family: Moraceae

The Indian fig tree, scientifically known as *Ficus racemosa* L., belongs to the Moraceae family. This is also called *Ficus glomerata* Roxb. The appearance of figs on or close to the tree trunk, termed 'cauliflory', is the unusual character of this tree. The tree and its fruits are known as *gular* in northern India and *atthi* in southern India. The term '*racemosa*' means the occurrence of flowers in clusters. The fruits are relished by the common Indian macaque. In Australia, this is a favourite food of caterpillars of the double-branded crow, a butterfly.

The Indian fig tree is a large tree growing to a height of 20–30 m with irregular crown. When the tree becomes old, it develops buttresses. The tree bears flowers and fruits mainly between September and November. Receptacles in large clusters on leafless branches become reddish when ripe. The edible fruits harvested from the trees are used as food as well as medicine.

The Indian fig tree is also known as cluster fig, country fig and *goolar* (gular) fig. This is also called *jagya-dimoru* and *mou-dimoru* in Assamese; *udumbara* in Bengali; *umbaro* and goolar in Gujarati; gular in Hindi; atthi and *atthi mara* in Kannada; atthi and *atthi-al* in Malayalam; *heibong* in Manipuri; *udumbar* and *umbar* in Marathi; *dimri* in Odia; udumbara or *hemadugdhaka* in Sanskrit; athi and *vellai athi* in Tamil; and *dumar* in Urdu.

Habitat and Distribution

The Indian fig tree generally grows near streams in drier areas as well as in evergreen forests up to about 1,800 m. This is a deciduous tree with a few aerial roots. This plant is frequently cultivated for its fruits and also serves as a shade tree in coffee plantations. This is a preferred ornamental tree in parks and gardens. This tree is found growing in southern China, the Indian subcontinent, Myanmar, Thailand, Vietnam, Malaysia, Indonesia, New Guinea and Australia.

Religious Significance

The Indian fig tree has been given prominence in the Atharva Veda as a means of acquiring prosperity and conquering foes. A hymn[*] extols an amulet of the udumbara tree:

> The Lord of amulets art thou, most mighty: in the wealth's ruler that engendered riches,
> These gains are lodged in the, and all great treasures.
> Amulet, conquer thou: far from us banish malignity and indigence, and hunger.
> Vigour art thou, in me do thou plant vigour: riches art thou, so do thou grant me riches.
> Plenty art thou, so prosper me with plenty: Householder, hear a householder's petition.

According to a Puranic legend, it is believed that Bhagwan Dattatreya lives in this tree. In Chaturmas Mahatmya, it is reported that this tree is the incarnation of Shukracharya, the

---

[*]AV XIX. 31

guru of the asuras. It is said that Lord Maha Vishnu, after killing Hiranyakashipu by taking Narasimha avatar, cleaned his nails on the bark of this tree.

In one of the stories of Raja Harishchandra of the Ikshvaku dynasty, it is described that the crown was a branch of the fig tree set in a circlet of gold. The *simhasana* (throne) was also made from the wood of this tree. The royal personage would ascend it on his knees, chanting to the gods to ascend it with him. The gods also did the same, although invisible. The leaves of this tree are used in fire rituals performed by Hindus.

In Buddhism, both the tree and its flowers are referred to as the udumbara. In Theravada Buddhism, it is believed that Konaagama, the twenty-sixth Buddha, attained *bodhi* (enlightenment) under this tree.

The Indian fig tree is worshipped as a sacred tree in 15 temples in Tamil Nadu. Lord Vishnu is named as Athivaradar after the name of this tree in Kanchipuram, Tamil Nadu. About 80 villages have been named after this tree, and 10 villages have been named after this tree in states like Andhra Pradesh, Karnataka, Kerala, Punjab and West Bengal. Many puzzles and proverbs have been developed using the name of this tree. Sundarar, the popular saint-poet, has mentioned this tree in Thevaram. Generally, men are named after this tree in Tamil Nadu.

Historical Significance

In historical times, both Hindu and Buddhist ascetics on their way to Takshashila (or, in Greek, Taxila), travelled through vast areas of Indian forests and used to consume the fruit of the Indian fig tree during their travels. In a gazette of the erstwhile

Baroda state, it is mentioned that the people of Gujarat had a strong belief that an underground stream used to flow under every Indian fig tree.[*]

Mythological Significance

Though Kanchipuram in Tamil Nadu is considered a centre of pilgrimage among Hindus all over the world, recently, the city became very famous because of the emergence of Athivaradar from the Pushkarani after 40 years. Hindus from all over the globe gathered here to worship and receive the blessings of Lord Athivaradar. There is an interesting mythological story discussing the association of the Indian fig tree with Lord Vishnu. According to the legend, once, Goddess Saraswati had a misunderstanding with her husband Lord Brahma, and took away his divine wand in order to stop him from performing the Ashvamedha Yajna in the Athi Forest located in Kanchipuram. With the support of the asuras, Saraswati, in the form of Vegavathy River, tried to interrupt the yajna. At that time, Lord Vishnu emerged from the holy fire, pacified Saraswati and helped continue the yajna. At that point, it is believed that Vishwakarma, the architect and divine engineer of the universe, carved a nine-foot-long body of Athivaradar out of a fig tree, after which, Lord Athivaradar agreed to stay in Kanchipuram on the top of the Elephant Hill.

Athivaradar is considered one among the four Brahma Kararchita Varadaraja statues, carved out of the Indian fig tree by Vishwakarma in Kritha Yuga. This statue was the main

---

*Mani, P.S., *Valam Tharum Marangal Volumes 1*, New Century Book House, Chennai, 1992, p. 39.

deity till the early sixteenth century. In order to protect and preserve the precious idols from foreign invasion, the idol was immersed inside a sacred tank named Pushkarani, which is at a secret location within the temple premises, and only one family, the Dhatacharya lineage, knew its exact place. After the two brothers belonging to the lineage passed away, the authorities had lost track of the Athivaradar.

In 1709, the water from the Pushkarani was drained out, and the Athivaradar was seen lying inside the tank. It was decided by the authorities to take out the statue every 40 years for pooja for 48 days and immerse it again in the tank for another 40 years. In another version, the idol was damaged, and hence, kept underwater as Agamas do not allow the worship of a damaged idol. Though it is generally believed that fig wood gains strength underwater, before placing the idol in the tank, organic preservatives are applied in order to avoid corrosion due to the salt content of the water.

Rising and Awakening of Athivaradar: After draining out the water in Ananthasaras, the temple tank, the idol of Athivaradar is brought back to the Vasantha Mandapam right on the main entrance of the temple with the support of 35 hefty men and kept open for the worship of the devotees. Previously, the Athivaradar had emerged on 1 July 1979, and before that on 12 July 1939. In 2019, the awakening and rising of Athivaradar took place on 1 July and continued up to 17 August. It is believed that when the Athivaradar emerges, he brings with him strength and prosperity that dispels darkness within and with-out. When the idol was taken out of the tank, it was dark, but after a few days, it turned somewhat reddish brown.

The idol was kept in a reclining position for the first 24 days and in standing position for the remaining 24 days.

Usage

The leaves of the Indian fig tree are eaten as a vegetable. Young shoots are eaten raw as well as cooked. The figs are edible, but usually full of insects. The fruits are eaten raw as well as cooked. The unripe fruits are also pickled and used in soups. The fruits can also be dried, ground into flour and eaten mixed with sugar and milk. The powder of the roasted fruits serves as a nutritious breakfast. The unripe fruit is pounded, mixed with flour and made into cakes. The liquid exuded when the roots are cut can be drunk as water. The tree's bark contains tannin. The latex is used to produce water-resistant paper. The wood is said to last under water and is good for well frames. Additionally, it finds applications in minor construction, inexpensive furniture, packing cases, mouldings, laundry tubs, fruit crates, and more. The juice is made into birdlime. The Indian fig tree is considered as the best shade tree for coffee. It grows fast and can be easily propagated by cuttings. This tree is used for stabilizing slopes, gullies and riverbanks as it produces a deep and wide-spreading root system. Its leaves are used for mulching.

The fig tree also has several medicinal usages. For instance, the leaves of the fig tree are used to treat diarrhoea. Its ripened fruit is used to pacify kapha and pitta and acts as a blood purifier. It helps control diabetes and relieves weakness. Decoction of the bark is used to protect teeth and gums. Cold

Fruits of *Ficus racemosa* at Makutta
Shot by Vinayaraj, https://tinyurl.com/2rpwzm28, licensed under CC BY-SA 4.0

infusion of the bark is an effective remedy for uterine bleeding. A fluid that exudes from the cut roots of the tree is used as a powerful tonic. The sap is applied locally to heal mumps and inflammatory glandular enlargements. This is also used to treat gonorrhoea. The root is chewed to treat tonsillitis.

Indian Fig, a Latex-Bearing Tree: This is one of the famous latex-bearing trees of India. The ancient masters of Ayurveda called the tree *ksheeravriksha* (latex-bearing tree). Based on its physical features and properties, this is also known as *hemadugdha* (golden milky latex), *jantuphalah* (presence of insects in the fruit), *kalaskandha* (black bark/wood), *yajniha*, *yajniya* (used for sacrifices), *srimana* (able to create positive thinking), *vipra* (wise tree), *sevya* (worthy of worship) and *pavitrakah* (purifier).

Cultivation Practices

Ripe fruits are gathered for collection of seeds. The seeds are collected by crushing the ripe figs in water. A kilogram may contain 600 fruits, which may have 2,200–2,400 seeds. The longevity of the seed is three months. The seeds are sown in nursery beds. Seedlings that are 5-cm tall can be transplanted into containers. Six-month-old saplings can be planted in the field. The fruits are edible and are considered a good remedy for diabetes. The Indian fig can be grown on the banks of water bodies, lakes, streams and rivers and in common wastelands. It can also be propagated through cuttings and air layering.

Peepal Tree (*Ficus religiosa*)

Peepal

Family: Moraceae

The peepal tree, scientifically known as *Ficus religiosa* L., belongs to the Moraceae family. '*Ficus*' means fig and '*religiosa*' means venerated. Its Sanskrit name '*ashvattha*' translates to 'under which horses stand'. *Bodhadruma*, another Sanskrit name, means the tree of perfect wisdom. As the tree has a resemblance to the poplar tree, it has been given the name poplar or pappel, a tree familiar in the northern latitudes. This tree is called *populo delle Indie* or the Indian poplar in Italy. This was known as the poplar-leaved fig tree in earlier descriptions of Indian flora. This tree is blessed with a very long lifespan of 900–1,500 years. This is reported to have been flourishing in its native habitat for over 3,000 years.

This is a large, deciduous or semi-evergreen tree without aerial roots. Generally, it grows to a height of 25 m and is often epiphytic. Its leaf is heart-shaped with a wavy margin and an elongated tip. This tree flowers in July–September and fruiting occurs in September–November. The fruits are small green figs that become purple when ripe.

The common English names for this tree are sacred fig, sacred bo, peepal or pipul. This is also known as *anhot* in Assamese; *asbattha* in Bengali; *piplo* in Gujarati; *pipal* in Hindi; *arali*, *aroli* and ashvattha in Kannada; *pimpal* in Konkani; *bodhivrikasham*, *aeri-al*, *arayal*, *ashvatham* and *arasu* in Malayalam; *sana khongnang* in Manipuri; pimpal in Marathi;

aswattha and *jari* in Odia; ashvattha, *bodhivriksha* and *plaksha* in Sanskrit; *arasu* in Tamil; *rai, ragi* and *ravi* in Telugu; and peepal in Urdu.

Habitat and Distribution

This tree grows in plains at an altitude up to 1,200 m. It is widely planted in villages, along avenues and near temples. This species is native to the Indian subcontinent and Southeast Asian countries like Bhutan, China, Laos, Nepal, Pakistan, Thailand and Vietnam. It was introduced in Sri Lanka in 288 BCE and subsequently in other countries such as the Philippines and Singapore. Introduced in Israel, it has become widely distributed because of the presence of its associated pollinator wasp in the country. Today, this species has been distributed to Africa, North America, Central America, Caribbean, South America, Australia and Fiji.

Cultural Value

Among Hindus, it is a common practice to use the twigs of the peepal tree while performing homam. Hindu women tie a red cloth around the trunk of the tree to pray for a child. As it is believed that Goddess Lakshmi sits under the tree on Saturdays, the tree is worshipped on this particular day to obtain wealth. There is a common belief that if one waters this tree, their children will benefit immensely. It is believed that installing a Shiva Linga under this tree and worshipping it regularly can bring materialistic happiness. It is also said that reciting the Hanuman Chalisa while sitting under this tree may help the concerned to attain a positive soul. People believe that if one writes 'Sri Ram' with *chandan* (sandalwood) paste on 11 leaves of a peepal tree and offers it to Hanuman, they will be freed from all obstacles and hindrances. It is advised to worship the peepal tree every Monday to have a booming business. It is also believed that chronic illness or diseases may be cured by watering and worshipping the tree daily. People hope that one's forefather's debts will be forgiven by watering the tree for 43 days, except on Sundays.

Religious Significance

In all the three major religions that originated on the Indian subcontinent, that is, Hinduism, Buddhism and Jainism, this tree is considered significant. Hindu hermits and Jain monks used to meditate under this tree as it is considered sacred. Hindus worship the tree by going around it seven times, saluting the king of trees. Gautama Buddha is believed to have attained enlightenment under this tree. Buddhists regard the peepal tree as the personification of the Buddha. The peepal tree is considered to symbolize enlightenment and peace. Bodh Gaya, where the Buddha attained enlightenment, is in Bihar, India. It is said that though the original tree was destroyed, it has been replaced many times. A branch of the original tree, introduced in Anuradhapura, Sri Lanka, in 288 BCE, is considered to be the oldest living human-planted flowering tree in the world, and is now known as Jaya Sri Maha Bodhi.

In Hindu scriptures, this tree is associated with the source of the Saraswati River. In Skanda Purana, it is mentioned that Saraswati originates from the water pot of Brahma which flows from the Plaksha tree in the Himalayas. In Vamana Purana (V.P.32.1-4), it is reported that the Saraswati rose from the peepal tree (Plaksha tree). In Rig Veda also, the same kind of report is found.

Tree worship on Saturdays and the tree marriage of peepal with bargad (*Ficus benghalensis*) is a special Nepali culture expressing their love for trees. Saturday worship is performed to please the planet Saturn. This is common among the people of Nepal.

The sacred fig is associated with the star Poosam in Hindu mythology. The tree is considered to be the son of Lord Maha Vishnu. In India, people consider this tree as holy and refer to this as Bodhadruma as this is believed to have the ability to enlighten the spiritual and mental faculties. People think that this tree releases positive energy. Snake gods are propitiated under the canopy of this tree in Kerala.

The peepal tree is worshipped as a sacred tree in about 50 temples in Tamil Nadu. Lord Shiva has been named after this tree and worshipped here. In Tamil Nadu, about 60 villages have been named after this tree and about 32 villages in states like Andhra Pradesh, Bihar, Jharkhand, Maharashtra and Odisha and Jammu and Kashmir (union territory). Proverbs have been developed in Tamil using the name of this tree as well. Both men and women are commonly named after this tree in Tamil Nadu. There is mention of this tree in Thevaram by the great saint-poet Thirugnanasambandar.

Sacred Fig, the King of Trees: Legend has it that during the Aswatha Narayan Pooja Festival, the sacred fig, revered as the king of trees, was wedded to the bitter Neem tree. This tradition continues in central India, where people plant the sacred fig seedling in temple premises and when it reaches adolescence, a neem tree is planted beside it. It is believed that when they both reach maturity, they are symbolically united in a nuptial knot during the festival. The tree is worshipped as Lord Narayana, and the Neem is revered as Goddess Lakshmi. In Maharashtra, even in modern times, people worship both the trees with the intention of begetting a male child.

Mythological Significance

This tree was used in Vedic times for making fire by friction. Since this is considered a sacred tree, it is rarely cut. This tree is associated with the Trimurti, the roots being Brahma, the stem Vishnu and each leaf being the seat of Shiva. In Ashvattha Stotra, it is said: 'I bow to the Sacred Fig Tree, to Brahma in the root, to Vishnu in the trunk and to Shiva in the foliage.'[*] In another legend, it is mentioned that Vishnu was born under the peepal tree and he is, therefore, considered the tree itself. In another myth, it is mentioned that while Shiva and Parvathi were in their private moments, the other gods eavesdropped. Enraged by their activity, Parvathi cursed them to be reborn as trees. As a result, Brahma became the palash, Rudra the banyan and Vishnu the peepal.

Brahmins offer prayers under this tree as they consider the peepal as a brahmin tree. In Gujarat, this is considered a brahmin tree and is invested with the sacred triple cord. The

---

*Prasad, P.V.V, et al., 'Medico-Historical Study Of "Asvattha" (Sacred Fig Tree)', *Bulletin of the Indian Institute of History of Medicine,* Vol. 36, 2006, https://tinyurl.com/2p9fz7m4. Accessed on 2 August 2023.

three-strands ceremony symbolizes the joining of a man, one woman and God into a marriage. It is said that the one who cuts the tree has murdered a brahmin, and his family will become extinct. When a male member of the family dies, the tree is offered food.

Certain communities believe that in the afterlife, the spirits of the dead do not receive water, and they regard this tree as a pathway to the next world. Hence, water is poured on its roots on three days of the dark half of Kartik (mid-October to mid-November), during Shravana (mid-July to mid-August), and on the fourteenth day of the bright half of Chaitra (end of March to April). Additionally, in West Bengal, it is believed that Manasa, the goddess of serpents, resides in this tree.

This tree is called the Bodhi tree or Tree of Enlightenment as Prince Siddhartha (also known as Gautam Buddha) received enlightenment under this tree; it is called *Samyak Sambodhi* or the Tree of Knowledge. There is a belief that the peepal tree is 2,147 years old, and it was believed that the ruling Buddhist dynasty would endure as long as the tree lived. Because of this belief, the tree was looked after with great care.

In the Purabi dialect of eastern Uttar Pradesh, there is a saying used to ward off evil spirits and describe someone's malevolent temperament. The saying goes: 'Jagdipa, who made the town desolate and from whom even the demon fled the pipal, is now coming with a pestle in her hand.' The story behind this saying is that once, there was a quarrelsome woman named Jagdipa. She was in the habit of fighting with everyone in the village. She used to abuse and hit them. As the lives of the villagers became unpleasant, they moved away from the village and settled elsewhere. One day, when there was no one left to quarrel with, Jagdipa picked up her broom and

Fruits of Pippala tree
Shot by Filo gèn', https://tinyurl.com/5cc24mt9

attacked the peepal tree. The demon who lived in the tree endured her torture for a few days before he finally rushed away and sought refuge elsewhere.

There is an interesting mythological story describing how Jarasandha's kingdom was saved by the peepal tree. King Jarasandha established a garden in Giriak, located on the northern border of the Ganga district. Due to drought, the garden began to wither. To resolve the issue, the king made a promise to give his daughter and half of his kingdom to anyone who could bring water directly from the Ganga and irrigate his garden within one night. The message reached the chief of the Kahars who were labourers in fields. So, the chief made a plan with his men. He constructed a magnificent embankment and created a long rope connecting the garden to the Bawan Ganga, a rivulet branching off from the main river. At night, his tribesmen dipped swing baskets into the water and sent them down the rope to the garden where the workers watered the plants in the garden. When Jarasandha came to know of this, he changed his mind. He did not want his daughter to marry a Kahar. He also did not want to part with half of his kingdom. So, he sat under a peepal tree and despaired. Suddenly, the peepal tree became a cock and crowed loudly. Thinking that it was morning, the Kahars stopped the work. Fearing the king, they left the place, leaving a small portion of the garden unwatered. Thus, the peepal tree helped the king save his daughter and kingdom. The king called back the Kahars and paid them three-and-a-half seers of grain for their night's work.

According to a Muria tribal legend of central India, the peepal tree was appointed as a guard by Mahaprabhu to protect all trees. In the beginning, Mahaprabhu made men, animals and other trees. As the number of men increased, they started making villages. Mahaprabhu made Chalika the king of men to maintain order, and Chalika formed a government to rule the region. Mahaprabhu appointed a chief and watchman for every village. When the population of the animals increased, Mahaprabhu appointed a king and watchman for them. One day all the trees assembled on Hemagiri mountain and complained of not having anyone to protect them. On seeing all the trees assembled on the mountain, Bhima, who was passing by, hurried to the top and asked for the reason. When they told him the problem, he wanted to put their strength to test. During the test, when Bhima pushed a tree, it fell over. This happened with all trees except the tamarind, the peepal and the banyan. Bhima informed Mahaprabhu about the test he had conducted. Mahaprabhu visited the Hemagiri mountain and appointed the tamarind as the king, and the banyan, with its widespread branches and aerial roots, as the minister, as it could collect information from every nook and corner of the Earth. Mahaprabhu requested the peepal to warn the other trees whenever the wind blew or a storm approached; the peepal thus became a guard. It is believed that the order of Mahaprabhu makes peepal leaves rustle in the wind.

Ecological Significance

The peepal tree may be advantageous for the environment, considering that it annually captures 2,252 kg of carbon dioxide (CO_2) per hectare and produces 1,712 kg of oxygen (O_2) per hectare.[*] By planting peepal trees in temple premises, government wastelands and on riverbanks, the adverse impact of climate change can be mitigated to a great extent. The central and state governments can organize planting of this species as a mass movement considering the ill-effects of global warming and climate change. About 500 peepal trees around factories may reduce sulphur dioxide (SO_2) concentration by 70 per cent and nitrous oxide (N_2O) concentration by 67 per cent. They also help to reduce noise pollution. Water management can also be improved upon by establishing ponds near peepal trees. Erosion can be controlled by planting this tree species on riverbanks. The pollinator wasp for this tree is *Blastophaga quadraticeps*. Many birds, such as parakeets, mynas, pigeons and house sparrows, act as potential dispersal

---

[*]Chalise, Anup Raj, 'Ficus Religiosa for Ecological, Ecomonical, Social, and Financial Sustainability Concept.' 17 February 2011, Ficus Religiosa Promotion and Plantation Campaign, https://tinyurl.com/34m5mrk2. Accessed on 2 August 2023.

agents. Mammals like bats, pigs, rodents and monkeys also help in dispersing the fruits. Thus, the tree not only provides food but also shelter to various birds, insects and other animals.

Usage

The fruits and leaf buds of the peepal tree are edible, though not tasty. As the bark contains tannin, it is used as a dye for cloth. A milky juice of the tree is used for making varnish. Gum obtained from the tree is used as sealing wax. Artificers, too, use the gum to fill up the cavities in ornaments. Since the bark is fibrous, it is used to make paper. The wood is quite durable under water. It is also used to make packing cases, fuel and charcoal. Elephants relish the bark and the leaves. Lac can be cultivated on the bark of the tree. This is planted also as an avenue tree.

The leaves and twigs are used as an antidote against bites of venomous animals and for treating fistula. Fresh sap from the leaves is used to treat diarrhoea, cholera and wounds. An infusion of the bark is taken orally as an anti-diabetic. A decoction prepared by using the bark is used as skin wash to treat scabies, ulcers and skin diseases.

Cultivation Practices

As the seeds of the peepal tree have a thick protective coat, they germinate successfully only after they are digested in the gastrointestinal tracts of birds and animals that eat the fruits. The droppings of these birds or animals can be collected and used to raise the trees in a nursery. The seed of the peepal tree may appear smaller than a mustard seed. It may take some time for the seed to germinate, but once it does, it grows into strong and healthy trees. The peepal tree is often propagated through cuttings. Of late, air layering and tissue culture techniques have also been developed.

Mahua tree (*Madhuca longifolia*)

Mahua

Family: Sapotaceae

*M*adhuca longifolia (Koenig), commonly known as *mahua*, is an important economic tree. The old scientific name of the tree is *Bassia latifolia* Roxb. This is also known as *Madhuca latifolia* Roxb. or *Madhuca indica* Gmel. The other species of this genus, found in Kerala and on the Western Ghats of Tamil Nadu, are *Madhuca bourdillonii* Gamble and *Madhuca malabarica* Bedd. Almost every part of the mahua tree has economic value, and hence, it is of great benefit to the people in whose neighbourhood the tree grows. In fact, such is the reverence for it that most villages grow it in temple premises, and even if a solitary mahua tree is found, the locals install an idol under the tree and worship it. This tree belongs to the Sapotaceae family.

Mahua tree grows to a height of 20 m with short and large rounded crown up to an altitude of 1,200 m. The deciduous tree with spreading crown can be seen in red soils, on hill slopes and along riverbeds. The hard wood is reddish-brown in colour. The tree flowers in March–April. The odour of the flowers may be unpleasant to some. The fruits are greenish and ovoid in shape. The fruits become reddish-yellow or orange on maturity. Fruits appear in September–November. The fallen fruits are enjoyed by children. Birds also relish the fruits.

The other names of the tree are *gudapushpa* (flower with sweet taste of jaggery), *madhudruma* (honey tree), *vaanaprastha* (widely distributed in the forest), *madhusrava* (honey dripping) and *swadhupuspa* (flower with sweet taste). Its English name is Indian butter tree. Apart from being known as mahua, it is also known by other trade names as *mohwa* or *moura*. The tree is also called *mahwa*, *maul* and *mahwla* in Bengali; mahua, *mohwa* and *mauwa* in Hindi; *ippi* and *alippe* in Kannada; *illuppa* in Malayalam; *mahula* and *moha* in Odia; *madhuca* in Sanskrit; *iluppai* in Tamil; and *ippa* in Telugu.

Habitat and Distribution

This tree is found in Madhya Pradesh, Maharashtra, Gujarat, Odisha, Uttar Pradesh, Chhattisgarh, Jharkhand, Andhra Pradesh, Telangana, Bihar, Karnataka and Tamil Nadu and on the southern Western Ghats. Even now, one can see the remnants of these tree groves in the vicinity of some of the famous temples in southern India. The trees planted along the roadsides of peninsular India have disappeared because of the expansion of roads in recent years.

Religious Significance

Mahua is worshipped as a sacred tree in the temples of Lord Shiva in Tamil Nadu, including Thiru Irumbai Maahaalam, Thiruppazhamanni Padikkarai, Thirukkodimada Chenkundrur (Thiruchengodu), Salem and Tirunelveli. It is also revered in the temples of Lord Vishnu found in Tuticorin and Pondicherry as well as in the famous Anantha Padmanabhaswamy temple in Thiruvananthapuram, Kerala. Mahua finds mention in ancient Tamil literature, especially in Thevaram, by the saint-poet Sundarar. In Telangana, mahua is considered sacred by the Raj Gond and Kolam tribal communities as the tree is associated with their gods and goddesses. In certain parts of India, especially in southern ones, almost every Hindu temple used to care for a grove of mahua trees. The oil extracted from the seeds of this tree was used for lighting the lamps in the temples. But, over a period of time, the groves disappeared, leaving only a few remnants here and there.

Mahua is worshipped as a sacred tree in about eight temples dedicated to Lord Shiva and Lord Vishnu. Thirty-two villages have been named after this tree in Tamil Nadu, as well as many others in Andhra Pradesh and Kerala. Many proverbs have been developed using this tree in Tamil too. The tree has been given special names by great Tamil poets of the Sangam period like Ilankeeranaar, Kayamanaar, Paranar, Kalladanaar, Maamulanaar, etc.

Economic Significance

In the past, the flowers of this tree were eaten as food, and an alcoholic beverage and sweet candy were made from them by the forest dwellers of central and south-central India. They would pay a fee of 10 paisa to one rupee for each tree to collect the flowers. They would clear the ground under the tree once flowering season started. Generally, the womenfolk were engaged in collecting the flowers. Later, they came to be collected and dried by men as well. Dry flowers may have only 50 per cent of the original weight of the fresh flowers. It was said that if a family with three children collected 64 kg flowers, it would fulfil the monthly food requirement of the family. The forest dwellers cook the flowers of this tree along with the seeds of *Shorea robusta* (sal) along with rice and eat it. Mahua can be grown on barren lands that are not suitable for cultivation. If planted along the roads, stream banks and grazing grounds, it may ensure the livelihood of the local people through collection of flowers and fruits.

Mahua Liquor: When there was famine in Bihar in 1873-74, thousands of people managed to survive by eating mahua flowers. It is reported that in the past, certain hill tribes were in the habit of bartering the sweet prepared out of the flowers for rice and salt. Even now, in Andhra Pradesh, the hill tribes are permitted to use 58 per cent of the flowers collected for domestic purposes. The beverage extracted from mahua flowers was the major alcoholic drink in the past in the states of Gujarat, Rajasthan and Maharashtra. Just as wine is relished by the French and whisky by the Scots, mahua liquor is relished by the adivasis of central and south-central India. The flowers are procured from central India to meet the requirements. In the last century, mahua flowers were exported. During 1883-84, the government exported the flowers that generated approximate revenue of 6.70 lakh. More than one million tons of mahua flowers are collected in our country annually.

Mythological Significance

In Indian mythology, the mahua tree is associated with the star Revathi, one of the stars in the almanac, and its presiding deity is Pushpa. It is said that the mahua flower is very sweet, soft, tasty and also provides a cooling effect. Those born under the Revathi star may also have qualities similar to that of the flower, like being sweet and soft-spoken with attractive physical features. Mahua occupies a major role at every stage and in every ritual of adivasi life in central and south-central India. The Gond tribe lives in some of the oldest landforms of India, the Gondwana. It is spread over Madhya Pradesh, Maharashtra, Telangana, Andhra Pradesh, Bihar and Odisha. A centuries-old tradition retained by them is their love and affection for mahua trees. The Gond tribe believes that the first Gond, Koya Pen, was born under a *koya* (mahua) tree. As it provides food, fodder and fuel to them, the tree is considered as the Kalpavriksha. Gonds celebrate Chaitrai Mahaparv during Chaitra, the first month of the Indian lunar calendar. After the *mahua tyohar*, or festival of mahua, celebrated exclusively in honour of their beloved mahua tree, they extract alcohol from the flowers. Usually, the festival is held before the rains. Pandum is observed not only as a celebration but also to maintain the biodiversity through sustainable consumption by not eating the fruits till they fully mature. This is because only matured fruits will have viable seeds that can develop into seedlings.

Mahua, the Tree of Life: As the mahua tree is considered the Tree of Life, it is never chopped down but passed on to the next generation. Since the yield increases as the tree becomes older, the tribes conserve it to reap an enhanced economic value. In Gond mythology, the mahua flower is considered rare and imbued as immortal as it never dies after drying. Once the flower is immersed in water, it comes back to life no matter how long it has been dry. In ancient times, when the tribal villages suffered due to epidemics caused by certain bacteria, they sprinkled mahua liquor to sanitize places of worship, dead bodies and boundaries of villages. The same practice is still followed in these villages. Mahua liquor occupies a major role in three important rites in their life: *tonda* (birth), *manda* (wedding) and *konda* (death). Post childbirth, the mahua liquor is applied on the navel when the umbilical cord is cut. The cord is kept immersed in the liquor and then buried. In Bastar village, mahua liquor is distilled to propose marriage. If the beverage tastes good, the proposal is accepted. The bride and the bridegroom are made to hold sticks of the mahua tree during the marriage ceremony. During the wedding celebration, alcohol is served to the guests. The place where the wedding takes place invariably has a mahua tree sprinkled with liquor. In death too, mahua liquor is found to be very important as it is believed that the alcohol transforms the spirit into a *pen* (supernatural power). After completing the death rituals, everyone drinks mahua liquor.

∾

Mahua tree plays a key role in the Adivasi ethos in Adilabad, Kumuram Bheem Asifabad, Mancherial and Nirmal districts of Telangana. It is worshipped as a sacred tree by the Raj Gond and the Scheduled Tribes of Kolam, not only due to its religious association but also due to its multifarious uses such as food, medicine and supplemental income, even during harsh summer months.

Before the collection of mahua flowers, *irup* pooja ritual or worship of the tree is performed. Mahua is an integral part of their mythology. As the liquor is sacred, it is offered to their gods and goddesses during festivals. Bada Dev or

Mahua fruits
Shot at the Melghat Tiger Reserve in Maharashtra by Dr Raju Kasambe, https://tinyurl.com/
ms5vc7sa, licensed under CC BY-SA 3.0

Persa Pen pooja is held before the commencement of an agricultural season, to seek blessings for a good yield. After completion of the rituals, the representation of Persa Pen (the supreme god in Gond mythology) is placed on the branch of a mahua tree till the end of the harvest in January. Before sowing of seeds, the marriage of Chanchi Bheemanna, one of their gods, is performed under the mahua tree. Totems of gods are made from the dead wood of mahua trees. The *dhol* (drums) used during the festivals of Ghusadi, Jangubai, etc., are also made out of mahua wood. All Gond festivals have some or the other connection with mahua. The tribals of Bastar in Chhattisgarh and people of Odisha, Santhals of Santhal Paraganas (Jharkhand), Koya tribals of northeast

Andhra Pradesh, Bhil tribals in western Madhya Pradesh and tribals in north Maharashtra consider mahua tree and the beverage obtained from the flowers as part of their cultural heritage. The liquor produced from the flowers is an essential drink for tribal men and women during festivals and other celebrations.

Uses

Mahua flowers are used for making liquor, jelly, sweet syrup, expectorant, etc. They are very good cattle feed. Pigs relish the flowers. Birds and wild animals like langurs, wild boars, jackals, spotted deer, barking deer, bears, etc., are fond of the flowers as well. The spirit obtained from the flowers is used to adulterate brandy in Europe. The hill tribes use mahua oil for cooking. Mahua fruit oil is also used for frying and manufacturing chocolates. It is used to adulterate ghee in certain places as well. Mahua butter or morwah butter obtained from the seeds is used as biodiesel. It is also used as a substitute for cocoa butter and ghee. Today, the oil is used for manufacturing laundry soaps and lubricants. Oil cake is a good manure and spread on lawns as a worm killer.

If proper attention is paid to raise and maintain large numbers of trees, thousands of people can be engaged in collection of the flowers and seeds, ensuring a decent livelihood. Wood is used for house building, ship building, building naves of wheels, turnery, etc. When raised on a large scale, mahua may help in establishing syrup and oil industries. Apart from industrial use, mahua trees play a key role in making locals economically empowered. As the leaves and the fruits are good cattle feed, it can be grown on grazing lands in villages. It can be raised as windbreak on private lands also. In addition to providing shade, the leaves and flowers become cattle feed. The oil obtained from the seeds is used to light lamps and for making candles. A study shows that the use of mahua oil blend improves engine performance and can be treated as a substitute for diesel.

This tree has tremendous therapeutic and potential use as well. Every part of the tree possesses some medicinal properties, either in small or large proportion. The mahua root, bark, leaves, flowers, fruits, seeds, oil and oil cake are known for treating ailments in Indian medicine. The leaves are used to treat eczema, wounds, burns, bone fracture, etc. The bark is used to treat rheumatism, ulcer, inflammation, bleeding, spongy gums, tonsillitis, diabetes, stomach ache, snake bite, bone fracture, itching, etc. The flowers are also used to increase the production of milk in women, as a stimulant, diuretic, etc. The fruits are used to treat bronchitis, ulcer, acute and chronic tonsillitis, pharyngitis, etc. The oil works as an emetic and an emollient and is known to cure skin disease, rheumatism, headache, piles, hemorrhoids, etc.

Cultivation Practices

The mahua tree grows in areas with not less than 750 mm annual rainfall. It grows well in sandy loam soil. It can be grown in clayey and calcareous soil as well. Through direct sowing of seeds or by raising seedlings in the mother bed, this tree can be raised. The seeds are to be sown immediately after collecting from the fruits. If stored, the seeds may lose their viability. One kilogram of fruits may have 450 seeds. Seeds are dibbled in raised mother bed. One-month-old seedlings can be transplanted into containers. One-year-old seedlings can be used for planting with a spacing of 6 m × 6 m. Initial growth is slow. The trees may start yielding from eight to 10 years.

Champaka (*Magnolia champaca*)

Champaka

Family: Magnoliaceae

Champak or champaka is a large tree found growing at high elevations in evergreen forests. The tree, classified as *Michelia champaca* Linn, has been renamed as *Magnolia champaca* (L) Baill.ex Pierre. This belongs to the Magnoliaceae family. Champaka tree has been named after the Florentine botanist Pietro Antonio Micheli.

Champaka is a large, tropical evergreen tree that grows to a height of 16 m and above. The grey bark is smooth. The heartwood is close-grained, olive-brown in colour and durable, especially underground. The sweet-scented flowers are found in white, yellow or orange colours. The tree flowers in May. The fruiting occurs in November–December. The fruits grow in clusters and have the appearance of grapes containing one to two seeds, similar to the size of pea, brown in colour. The tree is grown usually in temple premises for the fragrant flowers.

Though the common name is champak, it is also known as the joy perfume tree or yellow jade orchid tree in English. This is called *tita-sopa* in Assamese; *champa* in Bengali; *sachochampo* in Gujarati; *sampige* in Kannada; *pudchampo* in Konkani; *leihao* in Manipuri; *chompo* in Odia; *shenbagam* in Tamil; *champangi* in Telugu; and *champa* in Urdu.

Habitat and Distribution

Champaka, a large and umbrageous tree, is usually found in the tropical and subtropical moist broadleaf forests at an altitude of 200–1,600 m. It is cultivated in gardens and temples for its sweet-scented flowers. The tree is native to the Maldives, Bangladesh, China, India, Indonesia, Malaysia, Myanmar, Nepal, Thailand and Vietnam.

Religious Values

In Theravada Buddhism, it is said that the seventeenth Buddha, known as Aththadassi, attained bodhi under the champaka tree. Tibetans believe that the Buddha of the next era will find enlightenment under the white flower canopy of the champaka tree. As the groves are considered sacred by Hindus and Buddhists, they are protected in the southwestern regions of India.

Champaka and Mount Kailash: There is a mention of the champaka tree surrounding Mount Kailash in Shiva Purana. According to Vamana Purana, the flowers are used for worshipping Vishnu. The leaves are offered to Lord Shiva and Goddess Gowri on Nityasomavara Vrata and to Lord Vishnu on Vaikunta Chaturdhasi Vrata. There is report about the presence of the champaka tree among the fragrant and spiritually elevating trees surrounding the Bindu Sarovar Lake in Bhagavada Purana.

The champaka is worshipped as a sacred tree in about 15 Shiva temples in Tamil Nadu. This tree is revered as a sacred tree in temples of Goddess Kamatchi, Lord Muruga and Lord Vishnu as well. Eight villages have been named after this tree in this state. Both men and women are named after this tree. The champaka tree has been highly respected and praised in ancient Tamil literature by famous poets like Nakkerar, Kabilar, Seeththalai Saaththanar, Thiruththakka Thevar, Nalvazhuthiyar, Thiruvaalavaayudaiyaar, Nallanthuvanaar, etc.

Mythological Value

Champaka flowers are known for their unique fragrance. They are used for worshipping many gods and goddesses, though not including Lord Shiva. There is an interesting anecdote for not using the flowers to worship Lord Shiva. Once, the divine sage Narada visited a Shiva temple in Gokarna in Karnataka. He happened to enjoy the sweet fragrance of a champaka tree that was standing there. At that time, he noticed a brahmin standing near the tree. The brahmin had actually come over there to pluck the flowers. But, on seeing Narada, he refrained from doing so. When Narada enquired, the brahmin did not tell him the truth and told that he was attracted by the sweet smell of the flowers. After Narada moved from there, the brahmin plucked the flowers and hid them in a basket. When Narada returned, he met the brahmin there again. When he enquired again, the brahmin told the sage that he was going home. But Narada developed suspicions about the behaviour of the brahmin and asked the tree whether anybody had plucked the flowers. The tree replied in the negative. Narada was not convinced with the tree's reply, so he returned to the temple

Magnolia champaca flower stuns all.
Shot by Vinayaraj, https://tinyurl.com/2xmrtar9, licensed under CC BY-SA 3.0

and was shocked to see the Shiva Linga covered with champaka flowers. Narada asked a man who was sitting there about the offering of the flowers. The man told him that a brahmin offered the flowers daily. Lord Shiva was very pleased with the offerings and granted blessings to the brahmin. As a result, the brahmin became powerful in the king's court and started harassing the poor. When Narada asked Lord Shiva about helping the evil-minded brahmin, he replied that he was pleased by the offerings of the champaka flowers and helped him in turn. Narada returned to the tree, cursed it for lying and told it that its flowers would never be used to worship Lord Shiva. The sage cursed the brahmin to be born as a demon; the latter attained moksha when he was killed by Lord Rama.

It is reported in Bhagavatam or Bhagavata Purana that the *Vraja Gopis* (The Damsels of Vraja) used to ask the champaka trees about the whereabouts of the Supreme Lord Shri Krishna, the ultimate lover. The flowers are used for worshipping Lord Krishna. The champaka is considered to be one of the five flower darts used by Kamadeva (Manmadan), the god of love.

Usage

An essential oil called Michelia leaf oil is extracted from the champaka leaves. A yellow dye is distilled from the flowers. The leaf extract is toxic to the rice fungus, *Pyricularia oryzae*. In India, the flowers are used to worship in temples and are worn as hair ornaments by girls and women. The flowers are floated in bowls of water to scent the room and are also used to make garlands. The oil of the flowers is used to make perfumes. Joy, a famous perfume created by Jean Patou, is derived from the essential oils of champaka flowers. The flowers are also used to add perfume to clothes when stored and to add fragrance to hair oils. They are used for decoration purposes during religious and social ceremonies as well.

The timber is even more valuable. The finely textured, dark-brown and olive-coloured wood is used for furniture, carriage, building, house construction, plywood, tea chests, packing cases, superior quality boxes, battery separators, pencils, canoes, toys, cabinetwork, turnery, pattern making and carving. A kind of camphor is extracted from the wood by distillation. Special tests conducted show that the wood can be used for aircraft work as well. Vesicular arbuscular mycorrhizae (VAM) have been found on the roots of these trees. Soil under this tree has been tested to have a greater pH value, soil organic carbon and phosphorous. The tree is generally used to afforest badly eroded areas in Java. Butterflies and hummingbirds act as pollinating agents of the tree as they are attracted to the fragrant flowers.

Every part of the champaka tree is used in traditional Indian medicine. The leaves are used to treat swellings. The juice of the leaves along with honey is used as an antidote for infants' colic. The leaves are crushed and applied on affected joints with castor oil to treat arthritis. The leaves are found to be effective in treating intestinal worms. The paste or decoction of the leaves is taken internally for relief from fever. The flowers are used to treat nausea, fever and dyspepsia. The paste of the flowers is used to cure rheumatism. The flower buds are used to treat diabetes and renal diseases. The flowers are used to treat cardiac related diseases, leprosy and eye disorders. When consumed, the unopened buds are effective in curing gonorrhoea. The mixture of the flowers and leaves is effective in treating ulcers. The powder of the tree bark is used for fever and as a diuretic. Extract of the bark is used to treat diabetes related complications. The bark is found to be effective in treating tumours. The seeds are used for treating rheumatism and to heal cracked heels.

Cultivation Practices

The viability of germination of the oily seeds is poor. The seeds must be sown immediately after harvesting. Germination starts from the fifth week onwards and goes up to four months. Five-cm-tall seedlings are pricked into containers and allowed to grow in the nursery for one year. Saplings reaching a height up to 30–40 cm can be used for planting. Trees developed through seeds may take 8–10 years to flower, but trees raised through vegetative propagation may flower in two to three years. Generally, 3 m × 3 m spacing is followed. A rotation of 50 years can be followed to get quality timber. The tree is a light demander and susceptible to fire. Coppicing is found to be successful.

Mango Tree (*Mangifera indica*)

Mango

Family: Anacardiaceae

The mango tree, scientifically known as *Mangifera indica* L., belongs to the Anacardiaceae family. This is a large, evergreen tree extensively cultivated for its delicious fruits. This tree is considered indigenous to eastern Asia, Myanmar and Assam. The cultivation of the mango tree in India dates back to 4,000 years ago. It is said that the mango tree was found by Alexander's army when it entered the Indus Valley in 327 BCE. Representations of the mango tree are found on the stupa of Barhut and Sanchi dated 150 BCE. The fruits are a rich source of vitamins A, C and D. During 2017, when the global production of mangoes was 50.6 million tonnes, India stood at the top with a production of 19.5 million tonnes, while China produced 4.8 million tonnes and Thailand produced 3.8 million tonnes. According to the National Horticulture Board, about 1,500 varieties of mango are grown in India.[*] The uniqueness of the fruit is the distinct flavour of each variety. A universal favourite, the delicious mango is known as the king of fruits, and the fruit usually signals the arrival of summer.

The mango tree grows to a height of 30–40 m with a canopy or crown radius of 10 m. The trees live for quite a long period. It is said that some trees fruit even after 300

---

[*]'Ranking Shows Global Mango Production from 1961-2017', *Fresh Plaza*, https://tinyurl.com/3mwxjj2m. Accessed on 2 August 2023.

years. The evergreen leaves are orange-pink when young and gradually change to dark green at the time of maturity. The small, white flowers have a sweet fragrance. The tree flowers in January–March. Fruiting occurs in April–June. Generally, the fruit takes four to five months to ripen. Some of the varieties of mangoes found in India are *alphonso, banganapalli, neelam, sindhura, dasheri, chausa, kesar, langra, mulgoba, himsagar, totapuri,* etc.

The trade name of this tree is mango. It is also called *aamra* in Bengali; *amri* in Gujarati; *aam* in Hindi; *mavu* or *mavinamara* in Kannada; *mavu* in Malayalam; *amha* in Marathi; *amb* in Punjabi; *amra* in Sanskrit; *mamaram* in Tamil; and *mavi* and *mamidi* in Telugu.

Habitat and Distribution

This tree is found in evergreen forests, usually along streams. The mango tree has been grown in India since the Bronze Age, about 4,000 years ago. It was brought to East Asia in 500–400 BCE, introduced in the Philippines in the fifteenth century and by Portuguese explorers in Africa and Brazil in the sixteenth century. Later on, it was cultivated in Brazil, Bermuda, the West Indies and Mexico. North America, South and Central America, the Caribbean, Central Africa, Australia, China and South Korea are the other known mango cultivators in the world. Now, this tree is distributed worldwide and cultivated for its tasty fruits.

Cultural Significance

Mango is the national fruit of India, Pakistan and the Philippines. This is the national tree of Bangladesh. The mango occupies an important place in the culture of South Asia. History reveals that the Mauryan emperor Ashoka planted mango trees along imperial roads. The Indo-Persian poet Amir Khusrau has praised the mango fruit as '*Naghza tarin mewa Hindustan*' or 'the fairest fruit of Hindustan'. Sultan Alauddin Khilji enjoyed mangoes too. Babur has praised the mango in *Baburnama*. After his victory over the Mughal emperor Humayun, Sher Shah Suri planted the chausa variety in celebration of his victory. The famous totapuri variety, developed by the Mughals, was exported to Iran and Central Asia for the first time. While Akbar is said to have created an orchard with one lakh mango trees in Bihar, Jahangir and Shah Jahan helped in the establishment of mango orchards in Lahore and Delhi.

The mango fruit is considered as one of the royal fruits, along with banana and jackfruit in Tamil Nadu. Mango became famous in China during the Cultural Revolution and was considered as the symbol of Mao Zedong's love for the people of China.

Mango, a Wish-Granting Tree: Mango flowers are used for worshipping Goddess Saraswati. Mango leaves are used to decorate the archways and doors during auspicious occasions in the houses of Hindus. The popular Sanskrit poet Kalidasa composed poems praising the mango fruit. It is believed to be the incarnation of Prajapati, the Lord of Creation. In Hindu mythology, this tree is considered as a 'wish-granting tree' and a symbol of love and devotion. The Jain Goddess Ambika is usually depicted as being seated under a mango tree.

Religious Significance

In Hindu mythology, the mango tree holds a special association with the star Poorattathi. The captivating tale tells of Manmadan, the god of love, who used mango flowers as arrows to ignite the love between Lord Shiva and Goddess Parvathi. This enchanting theme has inspired mesmerizing poems and stories composed by both Sanskrit and Urdu poets. The mango tree is considered highly auspicious in Hindu culture and occupies a significant place in mythology, religion, rituals and customs. During festivals, homes and temples are adorned with festoons of mango leaves, adding to the festive atmosphere. Esteemed Sanskrit scholars in India have bestowed various poetic names upon this beloved tree, such as aamra (mango), *rsala* (juicy and tasty), *madhudhuta* (with a honey-like smell and taste), *saurabha* (aromatic), and *kamanga* (able to kindle love), celebrating its multifaceted beauty and symbolism.

The mango tree is worshipped as sacred in about 30 temples dedicated to Lords Shiva, Vishnu, Murugan and Goddess Kaamatchi in Tamil Nadu. About 125 villages have been named after this tree in this state and about 20 villages have been named after this tree in states like Andhra Pradesh, Karnataka, Kerala, Odisha and Sikkim. The mango tree has been praised by ancient Tamil scholars like Thirugnanasambandhar, Thirumoolar, Moovaadhiyaar, Tholamozhithevar, etc. There

are numerous proverbs and puzzles in Tamil which describe
the value of this tree.

Economic Significance

Greenery in an area can be improved by planting seed-origin
trees along roadsides, village wastelands, rivers, *poromboke*
(shared community resources) lands and on the banks of
ponds, lakes and canals. The tree, on maturity, may yield fruits
in addition to yielding wood. Considerable revenue can be
generated through this. The tree also serves as a windbreak.
When planted near houses, in the premises of big buildings
and in industrial campus areas, they can filter dust and purify
air to a great extent. Mango trees can grow well even in dry
and barren lands to generate considerable revenue. As there
is great demand for the fruits for making mango pickles,
drought-tolerant varieties also have been developed in recent
years.

Mythological Significance

The mango tree is considered sacred not only among Hindus
but also Buddhists. It is believed that the mango tree was
brought from Lanka to India by Hanuman. While carrying a
message from Rama to Sita, Hanuman leapt from tree to tree.
At that time, when he rested for a while on the mango tree, he
was delighted with the flavour of the fruit. The seeds thrown
by Hanuman into the sea reached India and spread over here.

Hindus consider the tree as an avatar of Prajapati.
Therefore, on all auspicious days, the twigs and leaves of the
tree are used by the Hindus. Traditionally, the leaves are hung

Close-up of a twig of Alphonso mango tree carrying
flowers and immature fruit
Shot by Ram Kulkarni at Deogad, Maharashtra,
https://tinyurl.com/5fatxcp5, licensed under CC BY-SA 4.0

over the doorways of the house during marriage ceremonies
and when a son is born.

Origin of the Mango Tree: The origin of the tree is described
in Hindu mythology. When an enchantress tried to persecute
the daughter of Surya Deva, she changed into a lotus flower in
a pond. A king wanted to have the flower. But before that, the
enchantress burnt the flower, and from the ashes of the flower,

a mango tree grew. The king took care of the mango tree along with the fruits. When the ripened fruit fell on the Earth, the daughter of the Surya Deva appeared from it, making the king realize that she was his wife in an earlier birth.

In ancient India, the bride and the bridegroom used to circumambulate a mango tree before performing the marriage ceremony. As the tree is considered to be sacred, its twigs are used in the sacred ceremony of homam. The flowers of the mango tree are offered to Manmadan. When Shiva was separated from Parvathi, he sat under a mango tree, and with the grace of Goddess Lalitha, he ultimately married Parvathi when he visited Mount Kailash. Therefore, marriage pandals are festooned with mango leaves. The mango wood is used in funeral pyres.

It is believed that the spirits of dead ancestors live in this tree. In 1772, Baji Rao II's father had murdered the Maratha Peshwa Narayan Rao and taken his throne. Baji Rao II suspected he was haunted by the spirit of Narayan Rao. So, he ordered the planting of thousands of mango trees to provide shelter to the angry spirit.

In certain tribal regions of India, the bride and bridegroom go around the mango tree many times before the wedding ceremony. The groom applies vermilion to the mango tree and embraces it. The bride also follows the same with mahua tree.

Uses

The tender mango leaves are cooked and eaten in Java and the Philippines. The dried flowers can be used as mosquito repellent. The unripe fruits are used for making different varieties of pickles. The ripe fruits are often eaten raw. Additionally, as the ripe fruits are very delicious, they are used for making jam, squash, jelly, juice, syrup, custard powder, lassi, ice cream, milkshakes, etc. The wood of this tree is used to make planks, doors, packing cases, boat building, furniture, etc. In the past, because of its dense canopy, this tree was planted along roadsides to providing shade.

The tender mango leaves are used to treat toothache as well as bleeding and swollen gums. The juice of the leaves cures sore throat and inflamed vocal cards. The decoction obtained from the leaves is used for managing diabetes. The bark is used to treat diarrhoea and indigestion. The tree gum is used to treat skin ailments like ring worm and itching as well as for healing cracked heels. Mango pulp, when applied on the face, helps to get rid of pimples and acne. The mango enzymes improve digestion and excretion. The presence of vitamin A in the fruit is said to improve eyesight and prevents night blindness. Regular consumption of mango is believed to strengthen kidneys, heart, brain, lungs and urinary tract. Mango pulp, when taken along with milk, increases haemoglobin levels and reduces anaemia. Regular intake of the fruit improves eyesight.

Cultivation Practices

Mango trees can be planted in pits of 1 m × 1 m × 1 m size at an espacement of 10 m × 10 m. Its planting should be done with the onset of monsoon rains for better establishment. Crops like groundnut, black gram, green gram, cowpea, etc., can be grown as intercrop in young orchards. Irrigation has to be given at an interval of three to four days for six months at the initial stage. One- to five-year old saplings can be irrigated at an interval of 10–15 days. Mango is grown as a rain-fed crop in major parts of the country. The fruits mature in three to four months from flowering. India accounts for 63 per cent of world production of mango. Of this, about 60 per cent is exported.

Bullet Wood Tree (*Mimusops elengi*)

Bullet Wood

Family: Sapotaceae

Bullet wood, scientifically known as *Mimusops elengi* L., belongs to the Sapotaceae family. *Mimusops* is derived from the Greek words '*mimo*' and '*ops*', which mean 'ape' and 'resembling', respectively. Roughly translated, the name means 'looking like the face of an ape'. As the flower of this tree resembles the face of an ape, this name has been given. The generic name '*elengi*' is derived from one of its South Indian names. This is considered as a prized collection in gardens because of its fragrant flowers. The flower of the bullet wood tree is the provincial flower of Yala Province, Thailand.

It is a large, handsome, evergreen tree growing to a height of 20 m, with abundant foliage and a round crown. The flowers are white and fragrant. The tree flowers in March–April. Fruiting occurs in August–September. The fruits are berries, ovoid and yellow-orange when ripe.

The common English names are bakul (meaning scented flower), Asian bullet wood, bullet wood tree, West Indian medlar or Spanish cherry. This is also called *bokul* and *bakul* in Assamese; bakul in Bengali; *barsoli* in Gujarati; *maulsari* in Hindi; *pokkalathu* and *ranjal* in Kannada; *omval* in Konkani; *anizham, elangi,* elengi, *mukura, bakulam* and *elanchi* in Malayalam; *bokul lei* in Manipuri; *bakuli* in Marathi; *anuradha* in Sanskrit; *magizhamboo, magizham, magadam* and *magizhamaram* in Tamil; and *kirakuli* in Urdu.

Habitat and Distribution

The bakul tree is found in evergreen forests up to an altitude of 1,200 m. It is found in ravines and semi-evergreen forests at an altitude above 500 m. Though evergreen in nature, this tree is cultivated throughout the country along roadsides, in temple premises and in homesteads. It has been distributed from India to the Malayan peninsula and has also been introduced in Hawaii, Northern Australia and New Caledonia.

Cultural Significance

The flowers of this tree possess honey, and the intoxicating liquor made of the flowers is said to stimulate sexual desire. Because of this, bakul is called by various names like *madhugandha, madyagandha sithugandha, madanath, madhupushpa*, etc. Ancient Ayurvedic scholars have given many other names like *sakesara, simhakesara* (presence of many stamens), *saradah, visaradah, saradikhah* (flowers that appear during saratkala or autumn), *surabhi* (sweet smelling), *bramarandhra* (liked by bees and beetles), *bahupatra* (abundant foliage), *sthirakusuma* (flowers persisting for a long period), *chakraakaram* (flower resembling the wheel) and bakul. According to legend, the tree is believed to blossom when graced by nectar from the mouths of enchanting women.

Religious Significance

In Hindu mythology, the bakul tree is associated with the star Anuradha (also known as Anusham or Anizham). It is said that Lord Krishna was fond of bakul trees. When he used to play the flute under the bakul tree in Vrindavan, on the banks of the Yamuna, the milkmaids were attracted to the sound of the flute. Bakul flowers are offered while worshipping Lord Krishna even today. The poet Kalidasa mentioned the bakul tree in *Meghdoot*. The medicinal properties of the bakul tree have been elaborately described in Charaka Samhita and Shushruta Samhita. According to Vamana Purana, the flowers are used for worshipping Lord Vishnu.

∾

Lord Shiva and the Bakul Tree: As per oral traditions, the bakul tree holds a special place in Lord Shiva's heart, leading to its widespread planting within the premises of Shiva temples. This revered tree goes by various names like Shivamalli (tree of Shiva) and Shivahalada (bestowing happiness upon Lord Shiva). The renowned Shiva temple, Vadakkumnathakshetram, situated in central Kerala, is celebrated for its vibrant Trissurpooram festival. This colourful event features crackers, drums and magnificently adorned elephants. Devotees of Lord Shiva gather at this temple, making it a significant spiritual destination. During the festival, a mesmerizing musical drum performance called Elanjitharamelam takes place beneath the canopy of the bakul tree, specifically conducted to propitiate Lord Shiva on his auspicious birthday. This unique offering adds to the festive atmosphere and holds a special place in the hearts of the devotees.

∾

Bakul flowers are offered to Lord Ganesha during the 21-pushpa pooja. In Jainism and Buddhism, these flowers are considered to be very sacred.

Mimusops elengi flower
Shot by Mark Marathon, https://tinyurl.com/Seazupnp,
licensed under CC BY-SA 4.0

The bakul tree is worshipped as a sacred tree in 40 temples in Tamil Nadu. Five villages have been named after this tree. There is a village called Elanjiyam near Thiruvananthapuram named after this tree in the state of Kerala. The famous saint-poet Sundarar has mentioned this tree in Thevaram. The poet Seethalai Saaththanaar has praised this tree in Tamil literature. Both men and women are commonly named after this tree in Tamil Nadu.

Ecological Significance

As bakul is evergreen with dense canopy, it can be grown for protection against pollution. This species is not only fruit bearing and ornamental but also has great medicinal value. Hence, it can be planted in village wastelands, gardens, homesteads and along roadsides. It can also be grown as windbreak. This species is found to be effective in preventing sand erosion in sandy areas and it filters dust. Since this tree has abundant foliage with fragrant flowers, it can be planted as an ornamental tree in front of major buildings and residential houses to have good shade and a pleasant environment. Bees and beetles are attracted towards this tree because of the nectar-bearing flowers. They visit the flowers to collect honey and enjoy the sweet fragrance of the flowers. Thus, bakul trees provide food to the bees, beetles, bats and birds.

Usage

The leaves of the tree are used as fodder for cattle in Odisha. Its fragrant flowers are used for making garlands. A perfume is distilled from those flowers. The dried flowers are used for stuffing pillows. The fruits of this tree are edible and used for making pickles. The oil obtained from the seeds is used for lighting lamps and for painting. This tree is also grown as an ornamental tree as well as to provide shade along avenues. Its bark is used for tanning as it contains tannin. The dye obtained from the bark is used widely. As the wood is very hard, it is used for building piles, bridges, carts, agricultural implements, boats, oars, masts, spars, rice pounders, crushers, oil mills, furniture, cabinets, panels, tools, turnery, picture frames, musical instruments and walking sticks.

The leaves of the bakul tree are used to treat headache, toothache, wounds and sore eyes. The smoke of the leaves is used to cure infections of the nose and mouth. The flowers are used to treat diarrhoea. The young fruits are used as an infusion for gargling to treat sprue. The pounded seeds are used to cure constipation. The bark is used to treat diarrhoea and dysentery. A decoction of the bark mixed with the flowers is used as a gargle to treat gum inflammation, toothache, etc. This is also used to treat gonorrhoea, snakebites, fevers, wounds, scabies and eczema. This is combined with tamarind bark and then used as a lotion to treat skin complaints.

Cultivation Practices

Seeds are collected from ripened fruits. Germination takes place within 15–90 days with a success rate of 90 per cent. Once a seedling grows four leaves, it can be transplanted into containers. As the initial growth is very slow, two-year-old seedlings can be readied for planting; 4 m × 4 m spacing can be followed. Watering is required for the establishment of the seedlings. This can be propagated successfully through cuttings, air layering and grafting.

Cadamba Tree (*Neolamarckia cadamba*)

Cadamba

Family: Rubiaceae

The cadamba tree, scientifically known as *Neolamarckia cadamba* (Roxb.) Bosser, belongs to the family Rubiaceae. Locally, this is known as *kadam*. The genus name is in honour of the French naturalist Jean-Baptise Lamarck. The sweet-scented orange flowers are used in perfumes. Generally, this tree is grown for ornamental purposes. This tree has great significance in Indian mythology and religions.

This is a large, evergreen, tropical and fast-growing tree. A mature tree may grow to a height of 45 m. The branches are spread out and horizontal. The fragrant orange flowers are in dense globe-shaped clusters. The tree flowers in May–July and fruiting occurs in August–September.

The trade name of this tree is kadam. The common English names are burflower tree, laran and Leichhardt pine. The tree is called *kodom* in Bengali; *kadamb* in Gujarathi; kadam in Hindi; *kadwal* or *bale* in Kannada; *attu tek, kodavara, chakka* and *kodam-bam* in Malayalam; *rajakadamba* in Marathi; kadamba in Sanskrit; *vella kadambu* and *kola aiyila* in Tamil; and *kadambe* in Telugu.

Habitat and Distribution

This tree grows in moist deciduous and evergreen forests along riverbanks at low altitudes in wet places of the west coast and Western Ghats up to 450 m. In India, this is found in the temperate Himalayas, Garhwal, Himachal Pradesh, Sikkim, Assam and Manipur. The cadamba tree is also found growing naturally in southern China, Bangladesh, Nepal, Sri Lanka, Cambodia, Laos, Myanmar, Thailand, Vietnam, Indonesia, Malaysia, Papua New Guinea and Australia. This is one of the preferred host trees of the larvae of the commander butterfly (*Moduza procris*).

Cultural Significance

The flower of this tree was the emblem of Athmallik State, one of the princely states of India during the British period. As per a Talagunda inscription c. 450 CE, the name of the tree is derived from the Kadamba Dynasty that ruled the state of Karnataka from its capital Banavasi between 345 CE and 525 CE. The Kadamba Dynasty considered the tree as holy. The kadam tree is associated with the star Chatayam, an auspicious star related to Goddess Lakshmi.

The tree is known as 'Kadamba,' as it has the power to pacify Vata (the wind element). The tree is also called 'Neepa,' for bestowing happiness upon living beings, and 'Vrittapushpa' due to its round-shaped flowers which are sometimes utilized by ladies as fashionable earrings. Farmers cherish it as 'Halipriya,' a tree favoured for use as a flavouring agent in agricultural practices. They even call it 'Bhalabadra' for its significance in cultivation.

Kadam Festival: The Kadam festival is celebrated by agricultural communities in Odisha and West Bengal. Ceremonially, the people of these communities plant the kadam tree on the eleventh day of the bright fortnight of Bhadra. Leaves of the sal tree, along with cucumber and vermilion, are offered to the kadam tree. Then they perform dance along with music. It is believed that this kind of worship ensures wealth and children.

Religious Significance

The sacred book 'Lalitha Sahasranamam' mentions the kadam tree, referring to 'Kadambavanavasini', one of the thousand names of Goddess Lalitha/Devi, symbolizing her residence in the kadamba forest. In the legendary 'Kalimardhana', Lord Krishna leaped onto the serpent Kalia from the Kadamba tree, earning it the name 'Haripriya', signifying Lord Vishnu's favourite tree.

This tree is mentioned in Bhagavata Purana. In North India, it is associated with Lord Krishna, but in the South, it is called Parvathi's tree. In Tamil Nadu, during the Sangam period, Tirupparankundram Hill, one of the six abodes of Lord Muruga, was considered as a centre of nature worship. Lord Muruga was said to be in the form of a spear under a kadamba tree.

Karam-Kadamba is a popular festival celebrated during the harvest period on the eleventh lunar day of the month of Bhadra by the Tulu people. A twig of the kadam tree is worshipped in every house and then young ears of grain are distributed among friends and relatives. Kadambotsava (the festival of Kadamba) is a famous festival celebrated annually by the Government of Karnataka in honour of the Kadamba

Dynasty, who ruled the first native kingdom of Karnataka. It is held at Banavasi, where the Kadamba kings organized the annual spring festival.

The kadamba tree is also related to a tree deity known as Kadambariyamman. Meenakshi Amman Temple of Madurai in Tamil Nadu was known as Kadambavanam in the past, where the kadamba tree was worshipped as sthalavriksham. A withered relic of the kadamba tree is preserved here.

In Sanskrit, the kadamba tree is associated with the monsoon. It is believed that the tree blooms only when it hears the roar of thunderclouds. The breeze that accompanies the rains is filled with the fragrance of the kadamba. This breeze is known as *kadambanila*. The rainwater that is collected in the hollows of the tree when it is with flowers is said to be imbued with honey. This water is known as *kadambara*.

As per Theravada Buddhism, Sumedha Buddha attained enlightenment under the kadamba tree.

There are eight temples in Tamil Nadu with kadamba as a sacred tree. This tree is worshipped as a sacred tree in the temples of Shiva, Amman, Murugan and Vishnu. Sri Kadambavaneswarar, the other aspect of Lord Shiva, has been named after this tree in Kulithalai, Karur district, Tamil Nadu. Lord Muruga, also known as Kadamban, is named after this tree. Thirty-two villages have been named after this tree in Tamil Nadu and there are villages named after this tree in states like Karnataka, Kerala, Uttar Pradesh and West Bengal. This tree has various special names in Tamil literature. Both men and women are named after this tree.

Neolamarckia cadamba flower in Bangladesh
Shot by Engr.Raju, https://tinyurl.com/5h7vskeh, licensed under CC BY-SA 4.0

Mythological Significance

The kadamba tree is popularly associated with Lord Krishna. The preferred theme of the Krishna-Radha legend, depicted in miniature paintings, is Krishna dancing with Radha and his beloved gopis under this tree. Till date, the tree is worshipped as sacred by followers of Krishna. In memory of Lord Krishna's swinging from the branches of Kadamba tree and delighting with the milkmaid of Brindavan, kadamba flowers are offered at temples of Lord Krishna.

Association of Krishna with Kadam: As per a Puranic legend, the exudation of liquor is associated with the kadamba tree. Sheshnag, the great serpent who supports the Earth, was roaming in the forest with his friends in the guise of a mortal. Knowing this, Lord Varuna requested his wife Varuni, the goddess of wine, to go and entertain Sheshnag and make him happy. Obedient to her husband's request, Varuni hid in the hollow of a kadamba tree in Brindavan as Madira. Krishna, while wandering in the forest, as Baladeva smelled the sweet fragrance of the liquor that the tree exuded, drank it with his herdsmen, and the gopis danced praising Krishna. From then, Krishna and the kadamba tree that supplied him with liquor have become closely associated.

According to Vishnu Purana, there were four sacred mountains, namely, Mandara, Gandhamandara, Vipula and Suparsva, with a kadamba tree, a *jambu* tree, a peepal tree and a vata tree planted on each one of them, respectively. Each tree spread over 1,100 *yojana*s (a yojana is a Vedic measure in ancient India measuring about 12–15 km) and towered aloft like banners.

Though it is said that sweet liquor exudes from the kadamba tree, it is not the tree but the flowers that yield the liquor. Kadambari, synonymous with wine, is believed to be named after the original kadamba tree that grew on the Gomantha Mountain, one of the mythical sacred mountains in Hindu mythology.

Once, Indra killed a harmless demon. This act of killing brought a curse upon Indra and, consequently, he wandered with no one to redeem him from his sin. After much suffering, Indra was freed through the power of a Shiva Linga in a forest. So, he built a small temple at that site in gratitude. At that time, in South India, there was a Pandiya king named

Malayadhwaja Pandiyan, son of Kulashekara Pandiyan, ruling a small city named Manavur, which was near this temple. The temple was in a forest with lot of kadamba trees and came to be known as Kadambavanam ('*vanam*' means forest). After knowing the power of the Shiva Linga, the king built a huge temple in the forest and developed the region into a princely state called Madurai.

Usage

The fresh leaves of this tree are used as cattle fodder. The leaf extract is used as mouth gargle. The extract obtained from the leaves is used to produce silver nanoparticles. The kadamba flowers are used in production of attar, an Indian perfume with sandalwood (*Santalum album*) base. The inflorescences and the fruits are edible. It is grown as an ornamental tree. The wood is used for tea boxes, planking, carving, turnery, dug-out canoes, plywood, light construction, pencils, match boxes, splints, pulp, paper and furniture components. This tree is grown along avenues, roadsides and villages to provide shade. It is one of the preferred species for afforestation programmes. The large number of leaves shed by the tree enriches the soil under its canopy on decomposition. The root bark yields a yellow dye.

The leaves of the kadamba tree are used to treat wounds, leucorrhoea, increased menstrual flow and to reduce swelling. The fruit is used to increase breast milk in lactating women. The fruit is also used to treat excessive sweating, thirst and burning sensation in the body. The bark is used to treat the infected wound, mouth ulcers, inflammation of the gums, diarrhoea, pimples, irritable bowel syndrome, fever, nausea and vomiting. The root is used to treat urinary tract infections and kidney stone.

Cultivation Practices

The kadamba seeds are sown in the nursery bed in February. The germination percentage is 60–90. Germination takes place in about three weeks. Up to 5-cm-tall saplings are pricked and transplanted into containers. Periodical watering is necessary. Up to 1 kg seeds can be used for raising two lakh seedlings. When the seedlings attain a height of 50 cm, they are ready for planting. Vegetative propagation through cuttings can also be tried; 5 m × 5 m spacing can be followed. It prefers moist alluvial soil, often along riverbanks and needs proper drainage. The trees can be planted along the boundaries of fields. While undertaking agro-forestry practices in inter-crop Kadamba plantation, ginger, turmeric, vegetables, pineapple, pulses, etc., can be planted alongside for three years. In Tamil Nadu, about 70–100 MT/ha after 6–7 years has been realized through seed origin plantation. This can be increased by 10–15 per cent through planting of site-specific clones.

Coral Jasmine (*Nyctanthes arbor-trists*)

Coral Jasmine

Family: Oleaceae

The coral jasmine tree, also known as 'queen of the night', scientifically named *Nyctanthes arbor-trists* L., belongs to the Oleaceae family. The coral jasmine flower is the official flower of the state of West Bengal in India. It is also known as the night-flowering jasmine in Kanchanaburi province of Thailand. Also called *parijat*, it is considered to be of divine origin. The tree is also known as the 'tree of sorrow' as the flowers generally open at night and drop off in the morning. The scientific name *Nyctanthus arbor-tristis* literally means night-blooming sad tree: '*Nyctanthes*' means night flower and '*arbor-tristis*' means the sad tree.

Nyctanthes arbor-tristis is a shrub or a small tree commonly growing to a height of about 10 m in deciduous forests. The fragrant, whitish flowers are produced in clusters of two to seven with orange-red at the centre. The tree flowers in August–September. Generally, the flowers open at night and drop off in the morning, which is why the tree is called queen of the night. During the flowering season, one can see a carpet of flowers under the tree in the morning. The fruits appear in November–February.

This tree is called night jasmine or coral jasmine in English. Other common names are queen of the night, night-flowering jasmine, parijat, *parijatham, pavahza malli* and tree of sorrow. This is called *sewali* and *shewali* in Assamese; *shefali, shiuli* and parijat in Bengali; parijat in Gujarati; *harashringara*, parijat and shefali in Hindi; *goli, harsing* and *parijata* in Kannada; *pardic, parizatak, parzonto* and *parzot* in Konkani; *parijatham* and *pavazhamalli* in Malayalam; *singarei* in Manipuri; parijata in Marathi; parijata in Sanskrit; pavazham, pavazhamalli and parijatham in Tamil; and parijatham in Telugu.

Habitat and Distribution

The coral jasmine is a shrub or small tree that grows in deciduous forests. It is native to the Indian subcontinent and grows naturally in certain areas in South Asia and Southeast Asia. In India, this tree grows in the outer Himalayas and is found in the tracts of Jammu and Kashmir, Nepal, east of Assam, Bengal and Tripura, and extends through the central region up to Godavari in the south. This is cultivated mostly for its fragrant flowers. Coral jasmine is also found in the Andaman and Nicobar Islands.

Mythological Significance

Since the flower drops from the branches with the first rays of the sun, it is the only flower that is picked from the ground and offered to the gods. Parijata, its Sanskrit name, means 'descended from the sea'. Harashringara, the Hindi name, means 'ornament of the Gods' or 'beautiful ornament'. This is one of the five trees that are believed to be present in Lord Indra's garden. Due to this reason, in Hindu mythology, the parijata is revered as one of the five wish-granting trees of Devaloka.

∾

Tree of Sorrow: The name 'tree of sorrow' refers to the flowering habit of the parijata tree, that is, it flowers only at night. Its name is associated with a mythological story. Once, a princess called Parijataka was in love with the Sun God. She tried her best to win his heart, but the Sun God rejected her love and, as a result, she committed suicide. A tree known as parijata arose from her ashes. For this reason, the tree is unable to stand the sight of the sun, and the tree flowers only at night and sheds its flowers like teardrops before the sun rises.

The origin of this tree has an interesting story associated with the churning of the ocean of milk. When the ocean was churned by the gods and the asuras, the parijata tree appeared along with Surabhi, the celestial cow; Varuni, the goddess of wine; apsaras, the heavenly nymphs; Dhanwantri, the lord of medicine; the Moon; poison; and Goddess Lakshmi. The story of the churning of the ocean has minor differences across various Puranas. According to Matsya Purana, the parijata tree is considered as Kalpavriksha, the heavenly tree. It is believed that whatever one desires under this tree, is granted. When the parijata tree arose from the ocean, it was taken to Vaikuntha by Indra.

Sathyabama, the third wife of Lord Krishna, once visited a parijata tree with a golden bark, copper-coloured leaves and fragrant flowers in the garden of Indra. On seeing the tree, Sathyabama became desirous of possessing it at any cost. She requested Lord Krishna to transport the tree from Vaikuntha. As he was not allowed to take the tree, Lord Krishna was forced to wage a war against Indra. After winning the war, it was taken by Lord Krishna to Dwaraka. Thus, Lord Krishna

Jasmine coral, a night-flowering jasmine,
has an orange carpel and pleasant fragrance.
Shot by Aashritha Kari, https://tinyurl.com/22jucxc2, licensed under CC BY-SA 4.0

brought this heavenly tree to Earth. Then, two of his wives, Sathyabama and Rukmini, wanted to have this tree in their courtyard. Following this, a quarrel broke out between them. To satisfy both of them, Lord Krishna planted the tree in Sathyabama's courtyard in such a way that the flowers fell in Rukmini's courtyard. It is said that the fragrance of its flowers spreads over three furlongs, and anybody who looks at the tree can recollect their past.

The flowers also mark the arrival of Goddess Durga. Rabindranath Tagore mentions the importance of parijat flowers in Durga Pooja in his poems.

Usage

The leaves are used for polishing wood and nail. The oil obtained from the corolla tubes is used for dying silk. The saffron-yellow dye obtained from the flowers is used to add colour to food items. The essential oil of the fragrant flowers is used as perfume. The bark may be used as a tanning material. The wood is used for fuel. This tree is widely cultivated as an ornamental tree in tropical and subtropical regions all over the world. Quite often, this is planted near Hindu temples in India, Sri Lanka, Malaysia and Indonesia. This can be planted and grown at the entrance of houses and in campuses of big buildings as it filters dust. Younger trees, up to three-years old, can be used to improve barren land.

The bitter leaves are useful as a laxative and diuretic. The flowers are used to induce menstruation. An extract of the leaves is given to children for the expulsion of roundworms and threadworms. The seeds are powdered and used to ameliorate scalp scurf.

Cultivation Practices

The kadamba can be grown even in wastelands with less rainfall. But it needs proper care. It grows well in fertile soil with nutrients. The tree prefers good drainage. This is widely planted in gardens and temples for its fragrant flowers. It can be propagated through seeds or cuttings. The kadamba has to be pruned annually to get more flowers.

Screwpine (*Pandanus odorifer*)

Screwpine

Family: Pandanaceae

The screwpine, scientifically called *Pandanus odorifer* (Forssk.) Kuntze, belongs to the Pandanaceae family. The Latinized term '*Pandanus*', derived from the Malayan word 'pandan', refers to all members of the screwpine family. Additionally, '*Odoratissimus*' denotes being full of fragrance. About 750 species of the Pandanus genus are distributed mostly in subtropical and tropical regions of the world. There are about 30–40 species of Pandanus spread over India.

This is a large, evergreen and gregarious shrub-tree. The stem is supported by aerial and branched stilt roots. It forms dense thickets on sandy coasts and tidal forests. The screwpine is found mostly near the coast. It is often planted along hedges.

The trade name for this tree is screwpine. It is also called *keyaor ketaki* in Bengali; *kewda*, *ketaki*, *keora* and *kewra* in Hindi; *mundige* and *kiyarige* in Kannada; *kaitha* and *thazhai* in Malayalam; *ketaki* in Sanskrit; *thazhai* in Tamil; and *mugalik* and *migili* in Telugu.

Habitat and Distribution

The screwpine grows generally at sea level at elevations up to 20 m but can grow at elevations of 600 m or higher. It is found growing along seashores, riverbanks, ponds, canals, etc. It grows in tropical climate and can withstand drought, salty spray and strong wind. The screwpine is widely distributed in

India, in the coastal districts of Odisha, Andhra Pradesh and Tamil Nadu, and, to some extent, in certain parts of Uttar Pradesh. It occurs naturally along high water marks at the edge of the sea and near coastal forests in Southeast Asian countries like the Philippines and Indonesia, and extends to Papua New Guinea and Northern Australia as well as all over the Pacific Ocean beaches.

Cultural Significance

The flowers of ketaki are given special importance in Indian culture. The fragrant flowers are used for making aromatic oils and perfumes. These flowers are worn by girls in their hair to win lovers. The Nair girls of Kerala avoid wearing the flowers as the tree is said to be cursed by Lord Shiva. There is frequent mention of the keora in Tamil classics as the flowers with their strong perfume neutralize the odour of fish pervading the coast.

Jehangir, in his memoir *Tuzuk-i-Jahangiri* mentions that the scent of the ketaki is so strong that it even obscures that of musk.

A wonderful Gujarati tribal song goes:

The sun rises behind the kewra tree
The moon applies antimony to its eyes
The night is lit with soft moonlight.*

---

*Gandhi, Maneka, and Yasmin Singh, *Brahma's Hair: On the Mythology of Indian Plants*, Rupa & Co., 2000, p. 43.

Religious Significance

There is a legend of how Brahma was denied worship and how the ketaki flower was cursed to never be used to worship Lord Shiva. At the beginning of the cosmos, a fiery Linga arose from the primordial waters and assumed a huge size. On seeing this, both Vishnu and Brahma were astonished and decided to investigate. They planned to find out its beginning and end. While Vishnu began digging into the Earth in the form of a boar to find out its lower end, Brahma flew high up into the heavens in the form of a swan to reach its tip. As the Linga kept on growing, Brahma could not reach the top.

Since Vishnu could not find its lower end, he returned to Shiva and bowed to him in the form of a brahmin. But Brahma did not give up his attempt and flew further. When he was going up, he saw a ketaki flower falling down. The flower told Brahma that it had been placed on the top of the Linga. Brahma forced the flower to bear false witness about his discovery of the summit of the Linga. After Brahma told this false tale, the all-knowing Shiva was enraged and cursed Brahma that no one in the three worlds would worship him. For giving false witness, the ketaki flower was cursed—it could never be used in the worship of Lord Shiva. According to Skanda Purana, Brahma was denied worship for this falsehood.

This tree has been discussed by the famous seventh-century saint-poet Thirunavukkarasar in Thevaram. This tree is worshipped as a sacred tree in the temples of Thiruchaaikkadu, Pallavanam, Sangavaneswaram and Anbil in Tamil Nadu.

Screwpine fruit (Kewda)
Shot by Razib Mustafiz, https://tinyurl.com/3x5zzcm5, licensed under CC BY-SA 3.0

Mythological Significance

There are different stories associated with ketaki in Hindu mythology. Its flowers are not offered for worship of gods. A story relating to this is narrated in Shiva Purana. One day, Lord Shiva was defeated in a game of dice by his wife, Parvathi. As he felt ashamed of his defeat, he hid in the ketaki woods. He undertook deep meditation to forget his humiliation. Sensing his feelings, Parvathi approached him in the form of a beautiful young woman and tried to entice him. As he was in deep meditation with his eyes closed, he did not feel her presence. So, Parvathi approached him wearing ketaki flowers in her hair. Lord Shiva was disturbed as he was attracted by the sweet scent of the flowers. Enraged by the disturbance, Lord Shiva cursed the ketaki flowers.

Usage

The trunk and large branches of the ketaki are used as building materials and for making ladders, headrests, hard pillows, vases and fish traps. Its trunks and branches are also used as fuel and for making compost. Prop or aerial roots are used in fabrication of house walls, basket handles, paintbrushes, skipping ropes, dyes, etc. The ketaki leaves are used for making mats, baskets, hats, fans, pillows, canoe sails, toys, etc., after proper treatment. The leaves are also used for thatching, making compost, cigarette wrappers, balls for children's games and ornaments. The young leaves are used for making fans, decoration and as pig and horse fodder. Preserved ketaki pulp, mixed with coconut cream, is used for making a tasty and sweet dessert. The flour prepared from the pulp is used for preparing a drink. Keys* of edible varieties are consumed raw or cooked. Juice and jam are also prepared from the fruit. During the fruiting season, adults may consume 20–50 keys daily. The fibrous, dried, mature drupes are used as paintbrushes, fuel and fishing line floats. The fruit is also used as bait for catching lobsters. The fragrant male flowers are used to add flavour to coconut oil, perfume cloth and make garlands. The roots are transformed into skipping ropes and basket handles.

There is also a very special use of the ketaki tree trunks. While the trunks of the female trees are hard on the outside, the interior is soft and juicy. After removing the soft interior,

*Segments of the *Pandanus* or screwpine fruit are known as cones or keys.

the female trunks are used as water pipes. In the Philippines, the leaves are cooked along with rice in order to add flavour. Meat is wrapped in ketaki leaves and grilled or deep fried to give it a sweet flavour. The pounded leaves are used to add flavour to cakes and sweets. As vanilla is to westerners, this flavour is a delicacy to Asians. The leaves are also used to make small containers for sweets, jelly and puddings. The leaves are wrapped around hot foods to produce aroma when the food is still warm.

The leaves and roots of ketaki are used to relieve general pain, headache and pain caused by arthritis. They are ideal for healing wounds. The preparation obtained from the bark is used to address skin problems and cough. The leaves are also used to treat leprosy, smallpox, diabetes, fever, ulcer, wounds, asthma, boils and cancer. Pandan flowers are used as laxative. The juice extracted from the roots of ketaki is used to ease chest pains. It is also used as tonic for women who have just given birth or women who are very weak.

Cultivation Practices

Ketaki can be propagated by offsets or division of suckers. The tree regenerates through offsets and start yielding leaves from the second year. While taking up hedge planting, linear bund planting is recommended. This tree can be propagated through seeds too. Germination may take about 2–3 months; suckers provide a quick propagation method.

Indian Gooseberry (*Phyllanthus emblica*)

Indian Gooseberry

Family: Euphorbiaceae

Indian gooseberry, scientifically known as *Phyllanthus emblica* L., belongs to the Euphorbiaceae family. This is commonly known as emblic myrabalan or *amla*. This is one of the most important trees in traditional and folk systems of medicine in India. The other name of this species is *Emblica officinalis* Gaertn. The specific name *Emblica* has been derived from the Bengali name '*amalaki*', and '*officinalis*', which, in Latin, means 'sold in the market'. This tree is considered as one of the precious gifts of nature to mankind.

This is a medium-sized deciduous tree growing to a height of 15 m. Its leaves have very small petioles. Its flowers are greenish-yellow in colour, and many male and few female flowers are found in clusters. The tree flowers in February–March and fruiting occurs in November–December. The yellowish and fleshy fruits are globose in shape.

The trade name for this tree is emblic myrobalan. Its common names are amla, gooseberry, emblic myrobalan and Indian gooseberry. This is also known as *amlaki*, *amloki* and amla in Assamese; amalaki in Bengali; *amalak* and amla in Gujarati; *brahma vriksh*, *bahu-muli* and amla in Hindi; *betta nelli*, *kaadu nelli* and *dodda nelli* in Kannada; amalaki in Kashmiri; *avalo* in Konkani; *nelli* and *nellikka* in Malayalam; *heikru* and amla in Manipuri; *avala* and *aanvala* in Marathi; *aula* in Odia; amalak in Pali; *manda*, *sudha*, *radha*, *amalah*, *vajram*, *tishya*, *akara*, *amalakah* and *dhatri* in Sanskrit; and nelli in Tamil.

Habitat and Distribution

Amla trees are found growing in the wild in scrub jungles, and dry and moist deciduous forests up to 1,500 m. This is found along hill slopes, on exposed slopes in dry and moist deciduous forests above 800–1,500 m. It is cultivated in the plains too. Amla is generally found growing in the Indian subcontinent, and South and Southeast Asian countries like China, Malaysia and Sri Lanka.

Religious Significance

In Hindu mythology, Indian gooseberry is associated with the star Bharani. Amla is regarded as a sacred tree in India. The tree is worshipped as Mother Earth and is believed to nurture mankind as the fruits are very nourishing. The leaves and the fruits are used for worship in Indian houses. The leaves are offered to Lord Satyanarayana on Satyanarayana Vrata, Samba on Shri Shani Pradosha Vrata and Shiva and Gowri on Nitya Somavara Vrata. In Himachal Pradesh, this tree is worshipped in the month of *Kartik* as propitious and chaste.

Amla, the Sacred Tree: According to legend, Goddess Parvathi and Goddess Lakshmi, while on a pilgrimage, reached Prabhasa Theertha, named after Prabhasa, the son of Dharmadeva and Prabhata. Agni Deva (the god of fire) resided in this pond. While resting on the bank of Prabhasa Theertha, Parvathi and Lakshmi planned to worship Lord Shiva and Vishnu. While they were involved in the ritual, tears of happiness spilled from their eyes onto the Earth. The amla tree was born from these divine tears on the day of Ekadasi. Lord Vishnu, Lord Shiva and the sages were very happy to see amla, and they called it The Sacred One like the *thulasi* and the bilva trees. From then on, both Lord Vishnu and Lord Shiva are worshipped with the leaves of amla.

In the Sanskrit Buddhist tradition, half of an amla fruit was the final gift from Emperor Ashoka to the Buddhist Sangha. This is illustrated in the Ashokavadana in the following verses: 'A great donor, the lord of men, the eminent Maurya Ashoka has gone from being Lord of Jambudvipa [the continent] to being lord of half a myrobalan.'* In Theravada Buddhism, this tree is said to have been used as the tree for achieving enlightenment by the twenty-first Buddha, Phussa Buddha.

Amla is worshipped as a sacred tree in 20 temples in Tamil Nadu. Lord Muruga is named after this tree as Nelli Vana Nathar in Virudhunagar district of Tamil Nadu. About 20 villages in Tamil Nadu and 40 villages in other parts of the country, such as Andhra Pradesh, Assam, Karnataka and Kerala and in Puducherry (Union Territory), have been named after this tree. Interesting proverbs and puzzles have been created in Tamil using the name of this tree. Both men and women are commonly named after this tree. This has been highly praised by the famous Tamil saint-poet Thirunavukkarasar in Thevaram. This tree has been given special importance by various Tamil poets like Kambar, Perunkadunko, Ilankeeranar, Mudavanar, etc., of the Sangam period.

---

*Strong, J. S., *The Legend of King Ashoka*, Princeton University Press, New York, 1983, p. 99.

A fresh haul of Indian gooseberries or amla
Shot in Pushkar, Rajasthan by Ji-Elle, https://tinyurl.com/36e2yrrt, licensed under CC BY-SA 4.0

Historical Significance

Athiyaman Neduman Anji, hailed as one of the most powerful Velir kings of the Sangam era in Tamil Nadu, was a contemporary and patron of the poet Avvaiyar (c. third-century BCE). Athiyaman ruled over Salem and the surrounding areas with his capital at Thagadur (now known as Dharmapuri). He was famous for his philanthropic virtues. The Pandya–Chera–Chola kings who were ruling during that period were jealous of his virtues and his kingdom's prosperity and planned to wage a war against him. Avvaiyar came to know about the plan and accidentally advised them not to wage war against a noble ruler like Athiyaman. She was one of the great scholars of the Tamil Sangam period and was treated with respect by every king in the Tamil region. Her words were regarded as the verdict of god himself. Her timely and scholarly advice was followed as a guide to rule the kingdom in a peaceful manner. Thus, the Pandya–Chera–Chola kings were successfully persuaded to stop the war.

After this, Avvaiyar came over to Thagadoor to meet Athiyaman. There, she was cordially welcomed by the Velir king who offered a gooseberry to Avvaiyar, and insisted that she accept and eat the fruit. After tasting the fruit, she realized the uniqueness of the fruit and enquired about it. The king explained that the fruit was specially blessed and those who eat the fruit would live longer. Surprised by the answer of the king, she said that it was the king who must live longer than an aged nomadic woman like her. When Avvaiyar asked the king why she was chosen to eat the fruit, he replied that she must live longer and serve the greatness of the Tamil language. It is said that Avvaiyar lived long after this incident. Thus, Athiyaman Neduman Anji also became famous by offering nelli (amla) fruit to the great Tamil poet Avvaiyar.

Usage

The leaves of the amla tree are used as fodder. The fruits can be eaten raw or dried. Wild animals like sambar and chital relish this fruit in forest areas. The fruits are also used in culinary dishes. Pickles are prepared using the fruits. The fruits are used in preparation of shampoos and hair oils. The branches are used to purify saline water. The wood is used for poles, implements, furniture, etc. The bark and fruit are used in tanning with the blackish dye obtained.

As the amla fruit contains antioxidant properties, it is scientifically proven to cure liver toxins, high blood cholesterol and age-related kidney disorders.[*] The fruits are used as a diuretic, refrigerant and laxative. Dried fruits are used to treat diabetes and dysentery. The fruits are also administered along with iron compound to treat jaundice, dyspepsia and anaemia. Seeds of the fruits are used to treat asthma and bronchitis. Since amla fruits are rich in vitamin C, they are considered to be effective in slowing down the ageing process. Amla is a major ingredient in the ancient Ayurvedic preparation of Triphala, which is a herbal formulation containing fruits of *Phyllanthus emblica, Terminalia chebula and Terminalia bellerica* in equal proportions. This is also a popular ingredient of *chyawanprash*, which is eaten by adults and elderly people. The amla fruit has acidic, bitter, sour, pungent and sweet taste. As this pacifies the three doshas, vata, pitta and kapha, this is called *Tridosha samana*. The fruit is used for treating all kinds of eye disorders. Amla is used as a memory enhancer, cardio-tonic and stamina booster and imparts youthful vigour and strength. It is used to treat nausea, haemorrhage, fever, cough, breathing problems, ulceration and leucorrhoea. It is also said to relieve thirst, burning sensation, impurity of blood and to promote hair growth. This is also used to neutralize snake venom and as an antimicrobial.

Cultivation Practices

Banarasi, NA 7, Krishna, Chakaiya and BSR 1 are considered popular cultivable varieties of amla. These varieties are

---

[*]Jain, R., et al., 'A Review On Medicinal Importance Of Emblica Officinalis', *International Journal of Pharmaceutical Sciences and Research*, Vol.6, No. 1, 2015, pp. 72-84, https://tinyurl.com/4sbw4wpa. Accessed on 2 August 2023.

preferably grown in dry climates in different soil conditions. Amla can tolerate salinity and alkalinity. Grafts and buddings are preferred to seedlings. Generally, planting is done during July–August with a spacing of 6 m × 6 m in 1 m cubic pits. Watering is required initially for establishment. No watering is needed during rainy and winter season. Subsequent maintenance of manuring and pruning of the trees are required for better yield.

Indian Gum Tree (*Prosopis cineraria*)

Indian Gum

Family: Mimosaceae

*P*rosopis cineraria (L.) Druce, commonly known as *jammi, shami, khejri, jand* and *ghaf*, belongs to the Mimosaceae family. This is also known as *Prosopis spicigera* Linn. '*Prosopis*' in Greek means obscure; '*spicigera*' is taken from Adrian von der Spigel's name, a physician of the sixteenth century. The tree is called golden tree or wonder tree of the desert. This is the national tree of the United Arab Emirates (UAE) and is commonly known as ghaf there. The people of the UAE are motivated to plant this tree to combat desertification and to conserve their country's heritage. In Bahrain, a 400-year-old ghaf tree called the 'tree of life' grows in a place where there is no water source at all. In India, this is the state tree of Rajasthan (where it is called khejri) and Telangana (where it is called jammi).

This is a moderate-sized, nearly evergreen and thorny tree. Its wood is very hard, dark brown and not durable. The flowers are small and creamy yellow. The tree flowers in March–May. Fruiting occurs in June–August. The pod may have 10–15 seeds embedded in sweetish pulp.

The common name of this tree is khejri. It is known as *semi* in Gujarati; shami, *sami*, jand and *khejra* in Hindi; *kabanni, jambi* and *banni* in Kannada; *parampu* in Malayalam; *shemri* in Marathi; shami in Odia; jand in Punjabi; *parambai* and *vanni* in Tamil and jammi or *chani* in Telugu.

Habitat and Distribution

The shami tree is tolerant of extreme arid conditions with an annual rainfall of 15 cm. It is known to tolerate high alkaline and saline soil conditions. Though the tree appears to be evergreen, it is found growing in the arid regions of West Asia and the Indian subcontinent, including Afghanistan, Bahrain, Iran, India, Oman, Pakistan, Saudi Arabia, the UAE and Yemen. It has been introduced in certain parts of Southeast Asia like Indonesia. The Al Ghaf Conservation Reserve has been established in the desert village of Nazwa, UAE.

Religious Significance

During Dussehra, this sacred tree is worshipped by the Hindus in different parts of India. Historically, the Rajputs, especially the Ranas, used to conduct a ritual worshipping the tree, part of which involved releasing the sacred bird of Lord Rama called Jay. In the Deccan region, during the tenth-day ritual of Dussehra, the Marathas follow the customary practice of shooting arrows at its leaves, collecting the fallen ones and putting them on their turbans. In Mysore too, the tree is worshipped on Vijay Dashami, the last day of Dussehra. It is believed that shami represents God Saniswara. Hindus worship this tree before undertaking an important journey and on the occasion of Dussehra. Religious Hindu women worship the tree regularly. In ancient literature, it is reported as representative of all 'F' factors: forest, fibre, fuel, fodder and food. Worshipping a shami tree is believed to be of great help in checking the damaging impacts of Saniswara.

∾

The Mahabharata and Shami Tree: The shami tree finds a mention in the Mahabharata, during the Pandava's thirteenth year of exile in disguise in the kingdom of Virata. Before departing for Virata, they kept their celestial weapons safely on this tree. When they returned after one year, they were happy to find their weapons safe in the branches of this tree. So, feeling happy about the safety of their weapons, the Pandavas thanked the tree for keeping the weapons safe and worshipped it for power to win the ensuing battle with the Kauravas. Subsequently, the Pandavas won the war and believed that the tree was capable of granting power and victory to those who worship the tree. Since then, Hindu warriors got into the habit of worshipping the tree before going to war with the strong belief that they would emerge victorious in the war.

The Ramayana, too, mentions that Rama worshipped the tree before going to war. Maratha soldiers were in the practice of praying to the tree, and accepting the leaf of this tree before proceeding to the battlefield. In Indian mythology, this tree is associated with the star Avittom, one of the stars in the almanac.

About 60 Shiva temples have the shami tree as a sacred tree in Tamil Nadu. This tree is worshipped as a sacred tree in the temples of Amman, Murugan, Vinayagar and Vishnu. About 20 villages have been named after it. This tree is highly praised in Tamil literature in different special names. More than 50 names based on the tree are used both by men and women Tamil Nadu. After the bael tree, this is the tree that is worshipped in the most number of temples. This tree finds a special mention in Thevaram, sung by the saint-poet, Thirugnanasambandar.

Historical Significance

The shami tree is popular in desert regions since it is capable of spreading in dry regions devoid of much water. This is also known as the king of desert. All the parts of the tree are useful. The shami tree has historical importance too. The Marwar (presently known as Jodhpur) region of Rajasthan was afflicted with severe drought in 1446. The drought continued for eight years, and the people suffered a lot. At that time, a spiritual leader, Jambaji, studied the reasons for the drought and established 29 principles in order to protect nature. The people who followed the principles were called Bishnoi. The principles prohibited the members from killing animals, cutting down trees and using wood for pyres. The Bishnoi community started growing a greater number of shami trees in and around their village. Centuries later, in 1730, King Ajit Singh was ruling Jodhpur. With the view to protect his subjects from the frequent Mohammedan invasions, the king wanted to build a fort. They were in need of firewood for the lime mortar kiln. The king was informed about the availability of a large number of shami trees in Khejarli village where the Bishnoi community lived. So, the king ordered his soldiers to bring wood from that place. Upon hearing that the soldiers had come to cut the trees, the villagers were very agitated. They pleaded with the soldiers and begged them not to cut the trees as they were their lifeline. At that time, a woman named Amrita Devi and her three daughters embraced a shami tree to prevent the soldiers from cutting the tree. The soldiers were merciless. The women were beheaded and the tree was

Indian gum tree fruit (*Prosopis cineraria*) in Tamil Nadu
Shot by Ajit, https://tinyurl.com/yhp5rc54, licensed under CC BY-SA 4.0

cut. Seeing this gruesome incident, all the other Bishnois started embracing the trees one after another. They were also beheaded and the trees were cut. The news reached the king, and he sent word to his soldiers not to cut any more trees in the village. But before his message reached them, 363 people had sacrificed their lives to protect the trees. Today, Khejarli village is a peaceful grove of shami trees including 363 trees planted in memory of the Bishnoi who sacrificed their lives. As shami trees are able to grow even in desert regions by sending their roots deep into the ground and the trees have multifarious uses, they are considered sacred by the Bishnoi.

Mythological Significance

Indian mythology narrates the story of Agni Deva, who hid in the branches of this tree in order to escape from the other Devas and from the curse of Sage Bhrigu. As the frog living in the ocean could not tolerate the heat generated by Agni Deva, it informed the other devas about him hiding in the ocean. Enraged by the act of the frog, Agni cursed it and hid in a sacred fig tree instead. An elephant that came to know about his hiding place informed the others. Agni cursed the elephant and hid in the branches of the shami tree. A bird noticed this and revealed it to other devas. This time, Agni cursed the bird and remained in the same tree. After some time, the devas finally located him. As Agni hid in the sacred fig tree and the shami tree, the Pururavas (a mythological entity associated with Surya and Usha [Dawn] and is believed to reside in the middle of the cosmos) generated the primeval fire through the friction between the branches of this tree and that of the sacred fig. Because of this, even now people use the branches of these trees to kindle the sacred fire.

Matsya Purana discusses the ritual of marriage with the shami tree. In ancient times, if a brahmin did not have a male child, he was allowed to marry twice. At the same time, it was believed that a third marriage would shorten one's life. Therefore, if a man was without any heir, he used to marry a shami tree. The shami tree was worshipped on Saturdays and Sundays as it represented the Sun along with his wife Chhaya. The brahmins offered raw sugar and boiled rice to the tree. The ritual was performed after formal greetings between the bridegroom and the priest. There were offerings of honey and sweets. A veil was drawn between the shami tree and the bridegroom and a ceremonious wedding was organized. During the wedding ceremony, a sacred thread was encircled around the newly-wed couple and tied to the groom's wrist, as well as around a branch of the shami tree. With the sacred fire lit, they worshipped Lord Vishnu, and the priest was offered two cows. After completion of the ceremony, the heirless brahmin was free to marry for the fourth time.

Uses

The shami tree plays a key role in the socio-economic development of the villagers by virtue of increasing the soil fertility, providing fuel, timber and vegetables to mankind. The pods of this tree are used as dry fruit in extreme arid regions of western Rajasthan. It is believed that if the growth of the pods is good, there will be a good crop year.

The green leaves of the shami tree are used as fodder for cattle. The leaves are relished by goats, camels, sheep and donkeys. In Rajasthan, it is a common practice that the leaves are collected once in five years. The shade-dried leaves are used as fodder for livestock. The leaves are also used as green manure. The flowers and buds are mixed with curd and eaten. The flowers are also useful for honey production. The pods are eaten as vegetables in Punjab, Haryana and Rajasthan. The Gond and Saharyia tribes of Madhya Pradesh eat the pods and the bark. Unripe pods are boiled and stored for lean periods in western parts of Rajasthan. It is said that the flour of the bark was made into cakes and eaten during the severe famines of 1899 and 1939. It is not uncommon that the bread prepared from the ground bark, with or without the addition of other flours, is also eaten. Dried seeds and leaves are ground and mixed with flour for making bread. As the bark has tannin content, it can also be used for tanning. The shami wood is used for making doors, windows, agricultural implements and for house building. The wood forms excellent fuel and charcoal. When planted in sandy areas, it helps sand-dune stabilization by preventing soil erosion. The trees planted in wastelands enrich the soil through the dried leaves that fall on the ground. The shami tree plays a major role in fixing atmospheric nitrogen. In general, this species plays a key role in the socio-economic development of the local people as it increases soil fertility, provides fuel, timber and vegetables to mankind.

The smoke of the leaves is good for eye troubles. The flower is pounded, mixed with sugar and used during pregnancy to prevent miscarriage. The bark is used to treat rheumatism, cough, leprosy, dysentery, bronchitis, asthma, leukoderma, haemorrhoids, muscle tremors, common cold and scorpion strings. The shami tree is generally recommended for treating snakebite.

Cultivation Practices

Ripe pods are generally collected by shaking the branches. The pods are dried in the sun and beaten to separate the seeds. One kilogram of pods may have 25,000–27,000 seeds. If properly stored, they may be viable for several years. The seeds must be soaked in boiled water for 24 hours to promote germination. Pre-treated seeds can be dibbled in containers. The seeds may start sprouting within four days, and germination completes before 15 days. Six-month-old saplings will be ready for planting. The spacing of 3 m × 3 m may be followed for planting. The younger seedlings are to be provided with support. When younger trees are lopped with minimum damage, they may bear lush green leafy fodder in the subsequent year.

Sandalwood (*Santalum album*)

Sandalwood

Family: Santalaceae

Sandalwood, scientifically called *Santalum album* L., belongs to the Santalaceae family. This is a threatened species, native to South India. This tree grows mostly in the Western Ghats and a few hills of the Eastern Ghats—Kalrayan, Shervaroy, Yercaud, Bodhamalai, Chitheri, Yelagiri, Javadu, etc., in Tamil Nadu. Karnataka is known for having a good population of this species. The tree is now owned by the concerned state governments. It was illegally cut and smuggled in the past for its aromatic wood, and, as a result, the population dwindled very badly causing this tree to fall into the 'threatened species' category. This tree is found in Pakistan and Nepal too. Because of its scarcity, sandalwood oil prices have risen to $2,000 per kg in recent years.

This is a small evergreen tree with slender and drooping branchlets. It is a root parasite and can grow up to 30 feet vertically. The seedlings live only for a short time. After that, their roots send out haustoria, which attach themselves to roots of nearby plants and grow. The sapwood is white and odourless. The heartwood is yellowish brown and strongly scented. The tree flowers in May–June and fruits occur in October–December.

The trade name of this tree is sandalwood. It is also called *chandan* in Hindi; *gandada* and *srigandam* in Kannada; *chandanam* in Malayalam; *chandana* in Sanskrit; *sandanam* in Tamil; and *srigandam* in Telugu.

Habitat and Distribution

The sandalwood tree grows from dry forests in the coastal areas up to a height of 700 m. Generally, it grows in sandy or well-drained stony red soils, but can withstand different soil types. This tree normally grows well in areas with an annual rainfall ranging 500–3,000 mm. This is native to southern India and Southeast Asia and is said to be cultivated first by the Austronesian peoples. Around 1500 BCE, it was believed to be introduced to the Dravidian people of southern India and Sri Lanka by Austronesian traders. Today, sandalwood is cultivated in India, China, Sri Lanka, Indonesia, Malaysia, the Philippines and northern Australia.

Religious Significance

The sandalwood tree is one of the five trees that are believed to be present in Lord Indra's garden in his paradise. As this tree is believed to have the power of keeping evil spirits at bay and to be one of the five wish-granting trees, it is worshipped by Hindus.

Sandalwood, a Holy Element of Hindus: The wood is utilized for worshipping Lord Shiva, and it is held in reverence as Goddess Lakshmi is believed to reside within the sandalwood tree. The paste derived from the wood is an integral part of religious rituals and ceremonies, adorning the deities and fostering a tranquil state of mind during meditation and prayer. Hindu devotees prefer applying the paste on their foreheads, necks and chests. The priests are entrusted with the preparation of

Fruits of *Santalum album*
Shot by Geetha Ramaswami, https://tinyurl.com/23me5uhd, licensed under CC BY-SA 4.0

the paste, which is used in temples and during ceremonies. The powder made from the wood, called chandanam powder, is commonly used in Nepal. After religious tonsure, sandalwood paste is applied, usually on the head of the devotees to protect the skin in all places, especially in Tirupathi. Sandalwood is believed to bring one closer to the divine in Hinduism and Ayurveda. Among Hindu and Vedic societies, sandalwood is considered as a holy element.

Sandalwood is an integral part of daily rituals in Jainism. The paste of the wood is mixed with saffron and used to worship Tirthankar Jain deities. Jain monks and nuns sprinkle sandalwood powder as blessings on the disciples. During Jain cremation ceremonies, sandalwood garlands are used to dress up the body. During the festival of Mahamastakabisheka, held once in 12 years, the statue of Gomateshwara is bathed, anointed with milk, sugarcane juice, and saffron paste, and sprinkled with powders of sandalwood, turmeric and vermilion.

In Buddhism, the fragrance of sandalwood is believed to transform one's desires into reality and maintain a person's alertness during meditation. The sandalwood scent is the most popular one used in offerings to the Buddha.

In Sufi tradition, sandalwood paste is applied on a Sufi saint's grave as a mark of devotion. This practice is followed particularly in the Indian subcontinent.

Chinese and Japanese cultures also use sandalwood along with agarwood as incense material in worship and other ceremonies. Sandalwood is considered the tree of life in Korean shamanism.

In Zoroastrianism, sandalwood twigs are used in fire temples during ceremonies, such as the Jashan ceremony. After completion of the ceremony by the priests, the attendees are permitted to place their own sandalwood pieces into the fire. Generally, money is donated for religious expenditures along with sandalwood. The price of sandalwood is higher in the fire temple than at the Zoroastrian store, as it is often a source of income for the fire temple.

Sandalwood tree is worshipped as sacred in about seven temples in Tamil Nadu. Two villages are named after this tree. One village is named after this tree in Gujarat. Interesting puzzles and proverbs have been developed using this tree in Tamil. This tree is highly praised in Tamil literature, especially in Thevaram by the famous saint-poet Thirugnanasambandar. Both men and women are named after this tree in Tamil Nadu.

Philosophical Significance

In the divine teachings of the Gurbani (Guru Granth Sahib), sandalwood as an example is used repeatedly. Sandalwood is known for its sweet aroma, and this fragrant nature of the sandalwood is symbolic of the Joti-Svaroopa, which is within the body as Infinite Bliss (*anand*). As the fragrance is within the sandalwood, similarly, the Supreme Being is the Inner Essence of all things animate and inanimate.

The same sandalwood can emit an unpleasant odour when it is left submerged in water. This is symbolic of man's submergence in Worldliness (*maya*).

The fragrance of sandalwood is compared with that of the divine virtues of godly people. When the lowly trees grow nearer to the sandalwood tree, they too become fragrant.

The Gurbani compares Nature as well as the association of Truth (*Sat*) with that of the sandalwood. As mentioned in the Gurbani, by remaining in the company of Sat, a lowly being is transformed into Divine Consciousness. The Divine Name is compared with sandalwood; it is calming and soothing just like sandalwood.

It is said that sandalwood trees are frequently encircled by poisonous snakes. But the sandalwood trees do not become poisonous because of their closeness to the snakes. On the contrary, it accommodates and tolerates the poison and remains fragrant.

The Gurbani suggests we become scented with the perfume of this Divine Name.

God's humble beings are also compared with the sandalwood tree. The sandalwood reminds us of our Joti-Svaroopa, and that we always have to remember the Divine Nature always.

Usage

The central part of the tree, the yellow-brown heartwood, is the most valuable part, which is used for its fragrance. As the heartwood is hard with oily texture and is durable, it is preferred for carving. The wood is used for manufacturing carved boxes, frames, fancy articles, etc. The paste prepared from the wood is used by Hindus, Buddhists and Jains in religious ceremonies. The oil extracted from the wood is used in perfumes, soaps, candles, incense and folk medicine.

Sandalwood oil is used in traditional medicine to treat headaches, stomach aches and urinary and genital disorders. The essential oil, emulsion or paste of sandalwood is used to treat inflammatory and eruptive skin diseases. In the traditional Ayurvedic medical system, the oil is used as mild stimulant and for smoothing the skin. The leaves and bark are used by Hawaiians for treating dandruff, lice, skin inflammation and sexually transmitted diseases.

Cultivation Practices

Sandalwood can thrive only with the support of a host plant. The sandalwood tree takes nutrients from the host plant through the roots and gets established. Pigeon pea, casuarina, etc., are the preferred host plants. Sandalwood seeds are soaked in water for 24 hours. The treated seeds are dibbled in the nursery bed. The bed is watered daily and germination may take place within 4–8 weeks. Seedlings with four leaves are transplanted into containers. One-year-old seedlings are ready for planting. Spacing of 3 m may be followed for planting. Sandalwood seedlings are to be planted within 1 m of the host plants. The host plants should be at least 1 m tall. Pruning of the host plant is needed if the height exceeds the height of the sandalwood seedling in order to provide adequate sunlight. The trees are watered periodically. The established seedlings need protection from herbivores.

Asoka Tree (*Saraca asoca*)

Asoka

The *asoka* tree is scientifically known as *Saraca asoca* (Roxb.) W.J.de Wilde and belongs to the Caesalpiniaceae family. The etymology of the word '*Saraca*' remains unclear. '*Indica*' means 'of Indian origin'. The Sanskrit name '*ashoka*' means 'without grief' or 'that brings no grief'. It is also called *pallavadru* in Sanskrit, which means the tree of love blossoms. It occupies an important place in the cultural traditions of the Indian subcontinent. The tree is valued for the fragrant, bright orange-yellow flowers that turn red before wilting. The population of this tree species is on the decline due to unscientific management practices, increasing demand for its bark, poor seed viability and over exploitation of its parts like bark, flowers, seeds, etc. According to the International Union for Conservation of Nature (IUCN), the conservation status of the tree is 'vulnerable'.

Asoka is a handsome and small tree. This is an evergreen tree with dense canopy. The wood is soft and reddish brown in colour. The pod tapers at both ends and has two to eight seeds filled with acrid pulp. The tree flowers in January–March and yields fruits in May–June. The trade name of this tree is asoka. It is also called *oshok* in Bengali; *asok* in Hindi; asoka and *ashunkar* in Kannada; *asokam* in Malayalam; ashoka, *Sita ashoka*, pallavadru and *karkeli* in Sanskrit; asoka and *asavu* in Tamil; and *ashokmu* and *vanjulamu* in Telugu.

Habitat and Distribution

Asoka is found growing in evergreen, climax forests of the Western Ghats and in the Deccan Plateau of the Indian subcontinent. The tree is becoming rarer in its original habitats. However, isolated trees are found in the foothills of the central and eastern Himalayas up to an altitude of 750 m in the northern plains of India and on the west coast of the subcontinent near Mumbai. This is found in large numbers in Sri Lanka, Malaysia and Myanmar. Thomas Fulton Bourdillon, the conservator of forests in the erstwhile princely state of Travancore, in a report prepared in 1908, mentioned the existence of asoka trees on both sides of the road from Puliyarai (Tirunelveli district of Tamil Nadu) up to Ariyankavu (Kerala).[*] Bees, moths, white ants, black ants and butterflies play a key role in cross pollination of this tree species.

Religious Significance

The asoka tree is considered sacred all over India, Nepal and Sri Lanka. The tree is portrayed in many religions and literature. Because of its handsome appearance and brightly coloured flowers, it is found in the gardens of palaces and premises of temples in India. Kamadeva, the god of love, is said to have included asoka blossoms among the five flowers in his quiver. Vamana Purana recommends using asoka flowers for worship. The flowers are used to decorate temples. Asoka flower buds are eaten in Bengal during *Sashti*, the sixth day

---

*Mani, P.S., *Valam Tharum Marangal Volumes 1*, New Century Book House, Chennai, 1992, p. 24.

of the bright fortnight of the month of Baisakh (April–May). When Sita was abducted by Ravana, she stayed under this tree in Ashoka Vatika. It is believed that Sita was able to overcome her grief by staying under the asoka tree. So, it is considered to be auspicious to plant the tree within the premises or near houses as the tree is believed to remove sorrow.

The tree holds great popularity in the Mathura school of sculpture, often depicted surrounded by female figures known as Vrikshadevatas or tree deities representing fertility, revered by childless women.

The asoka tree is believed to be sacred in Hinduism, Buddhism and Jainism. The tree is described as auspicious in Ramayana. The Chinese traveller Hiuen Tsang, who visited India in 630 CE, reported seeing the asoka tree under which the birth took place. Around 250 BCE, Prince Mahendra, Emperor Ashoka's son, brought a sapling of the tree to Ceylon and planted it in Anuradhapur. Today, the ancient tree's massive branches are supported by pillars, making it the world's oldest historically significant tree. Mahavira is believed to have renounced the world under an asoka tree in Vaishali, according to the Jain tradition.

Mythological Significance

In India, the trees are considered like human beings, as if blessed with a soul and a heart that weeps with grief and laughs with joy. It is believed that they have feelings and aspirations like mankind. There is a strong belief among Hindus that the one who eats eight buds of asoka flowers in the month of Chaitra, suffers no bereavements in life. In Indian literature, there are instances where the asoka tree is addressed as if it is alive and has feelings. In the Mahabharata, Damayanti, while looking for Nala, goes to the forest of the asoka trees and pleads with a tree to free her from grief. In India, Hindus worship the tree on the thirteenth day of the month of Chaitra.

Asoka, Sacred to Shiva: As Goddess Parvathi had worshipped Lord Shiva with the flowers of this tree, it was blessed by Lord Shiva to be immortal and, because of this, the tree is believed to remain evergreen. The orange-red flowers of this tree are offered for worshipping. It is believed that the tree will flower only if grown on ground trodden by a chaste woman. There is another strange belief that the tree blossoms only when kicked by a young virgin. A young forest maiden is very often depicted in sculpture kicking the trunk of an asoka tree which then flowers profusely. The tree is considered to be sacred to Lord Shiva and is planted on the southeast corner of temples.

There is an interesting myth in Bhavishya Purana. According to it, years before the abduction of Sita by Ravana, there lived a person named Sashoka. He happened to be a cannibal by birth, but later repented for his lifestyle and wanted to change. So, he approached a hermit who advised him to perform prayers and penance for the rest of his life. Then he would be reborn as a tree in Ravana's garden, and Sita would take refuge under the tree. When Hanuman tried to console Sita sitting on the tree, her sorrow would disappear. Then the sins of Sashoka would be washed away and all would come to know of the tree as the asoka, the one which removes grief.

As the asoka tree is closely associated with Yakshi

Saraca asoca flowers in full bloom in Kerala
Shot by Vinayaraj, https://tinyurl.com/3h4w25ek,
licensed under CC BY-SA 4.0

mythological beings, this tree is often found at the gates of Buddhist and Hindu temples. The Yakshis under this tree were very popular as decorative elements in ancient Buddhist monuments. The tree is portrayed in ancient religious and amorous poetry and has sixteen different names in Sanskrit mentioning its different parts.

Usage

Asoka is an ornamental tree. The pods are used as fodder for cattle. The seeds are eaten by Karbi tribe of Assam. The bark has a sour and bitter taste. It is peeled off in vertical strips with 6 cm spacing between each strip. In one or two years, the peeled-off area is renewed with fresh bark. The bark is shade dried, packed and stored in containers for sale. Annually, 300 metric tonnes of bark are collected and sold in the central Indian region. The wood is soft and used for making agricultural implements and building materials. It is believed that planting of asoka trees at home spreads positive energy.

Medicinal Usage

Each part of the tree has medicinal value and cures many ailments. The medicine prepared by using the leaves, flowers and bark is used to treat diarrhoea and purify the blood. The juice extracted from the flowers is used to cure dysentery. Dried flowers are used to treat diabetes and indigestion. The flowers are effective in maintaining blood sugar levels. Water mixed with crushed flowers prevents internal bleeding. Bark or leaves, when consumed, remove worms from the stomach and provide relief from pain and swelling.

As the bark contains anti-fungal, anti-bacterial and pain-relieving properties, it helps treat both internal and external inflammation and provides relief from burning sensation. A decoction prepared from the bark is used to treat internal piles. Seed powder is used to prevent kidney stones. Consumption of seed powder wrapped with betel leaves helps to cure asthma. The paste of the bark is used to treat joint pains. Cosmetics prepared from the bark help to improve the skin complexion. The medicine prepared from the bark is used to treat scorpion bite. The decoction prepared by boiling the bark along with mustard oil is found beneficial to treat boils and acne. The extract of this tree is used to treat irregular menstrual cycles, amenorrhea, leucorrhoea, cysts and other such disorders. As the tree is used to treat gynaecological and menstrual problems in women, the tree is known to be women friendly. Regular consumption of asoka bark and *brahmi* powder mixed in equal ratio along with milk is said to boost memory. The extract of the tree is used to treat skin disorders thus helping to cure burn and skin irritations. Pregnant women should not consume products from this tree as it may lead to complications.

Cultivation Practices

Mature pods are collected directly from the trees and the seeds are obtained after shade-drying the pods. Since the viability of the seeds is poor, the seeds are to be sown immediately after collection. They are to be soaked in water for 12 hours before sowing in order to improve the germination percentage. The seeds are sown in mother beds. They germinate in about 15 days. Seedlings with four leaves are transplanted into containers. One-year-old seedlings are planted in 45 cm cubic pits at an espacement of 8 m × 8 m along the roads and 6 m × 6 m within the premises of the buildings. The tree flowers at 6–8 years of age and yields fruits in July–October. The tree survives for about 50 years.

Original and False Asoka Tree: *Polyalthia longifolia* is also called the mast tree or the Indian fir. '*Polyalthia*' in Greek means 'of many cures', while '*longifolia*' in Latin refers to the length of its leaves. Many people mistake the mast tree for the asoka tree, and because of its physical resemblance to the asoka tree, it is known as 'false asoka'. The asoka can be easily differentiated from the false asoka–the asoka has a bigger canopy and red blooms.

Sal Tree (*Shorea robusta*)

Sal

Family: Dipterocarpaceae

The *sal* tree, scientifically known as *Shorea robusta* C.F. Gaertn, belongs to the Dipterocarpaceae family. '*Shorea*' shares its origins with the name of Dr Charles W. Shore, a botanist from Kentucky, USA. '*Robusta*' means stout. This is the state tree of two Indian states, Chhattisgarh and Jharkhand.

Sal is a large and gregarious tree, growing up to 30–35 m tall. In wetter areas, sal is evergreen; in drier areas, it is dry-deciduous, shedding most of the leaves between February and April and sprouting again in April and May. This tree flowers in March and fruiting occurs in June. The fruit is ovoid and each has one seed. Sal is the most important hardwood timber in India.

This tree is also known as sal and *hal* in Assamese; sal in Bengali; sal, *salwa*, *sakhu* and *sakher* in Hindi; *ashvakarna*, *asina*, *asu* and *bile-bhogimara* in Kannada; *karimaruthu*, *kungiliyam* and *maramaram* in Malayalam; sal, *guggilu*, *rala* and *sajara* in Marathi; *sargi gatcho* in Odia; *agnivallabha*, *ashvakarna* and *ashvakarnika* in Sanskrit; *venkungiliyam*, *kungiliyam* and *saluvai maram* in Tamil; and *ral* and *safed dammer* in Urdu. It is commonly called Indian dammer.

Habitat and Distribution

The sal tree is native to the Indian subcontinent, ranging south of the Himalayas, from Myanmar in the east to Nepal, India and Bangladesh. This tree is the dominant species in the forests of the sub-Himalayan tract. In Nepal, in protected areas like Chitwan National Park, Bardia National Park and Shukla Phat Wildlife Reserve, there are dense forests of huge sal trees. It is a rare tree in China, but it is gregarious in savannah woodlands at elevations below 800 m in southeastern Xizang. This is considered the main tree in the forests of Nepal at elevations up to 1,400 m.

Religious Significance

As per ancient Indian literature, the sal tree is said to be the favourite of Lord Maha Vishnu. The tree finds a place in the Ramayana, when Lord Rama is requested to pierce seven sal trees in a row with a single arrow—an arrow that is later used to kill Vali, Sugreeva's older half-brother, and also to behead Ravana's brother Kumbhakarna.

It is stated in Jainism that the twenty-fourth Tirthankara, Mahavira, achieved enlightenment under a sal tree. The Bagadis and Bauris of Bengal worship Sarna Burthi, a goddess associated with sacred groves of sal trees. In the Kathmandu valley in Nepal, temples such as Nyatapol are made of bricks and sal wood.

Gautama Buddha and the Sal Tree: It is believed in Buddhist tradition that Queen Maya of the Sakya clan, on her way to her grandfather's kingdom, gave birth to Gautama Buddha by grasping the branch of a sal tree in a garden in Lumbini in south Nepal. It is reported in Buddhist tradition that the Buddha was lying between a pair of sal trees when he died. It is said that when a large community of monks visited the Buddha on the shore of the Hirannavati River, he requested his disciple Ananda to prepare a bed for him between the twin sal trees with his head to the north so he could lie down as he was tired.

According to Buddhist tradition, Kondanna and Vessabhu, the fifth and twenty-fourth Buddhas preceding Gautama Buddha, respectively, attained enlightenment under the sal tree. In Buddhism, the brief flowering of the sal tree is used as a symbol of impermanence and of rapid passing glory. In Japanese Buddhism, this is best explained in the tale of the rise and fall of a once-powerful clan; a line from the story reads, 'the colour of the sal flowers reveals the truth that the prosperous must decline.' This is reiterated by quoting from a passage in the Humane King Sutra, 'The prosperous inevitably decline, the full inevitably empty.'

Mythological Significance

A folk tale from Gujarat describes the sacredness of the sal tree. According to the tale, there is a shrine of Bhimanatha Mahadeva in Baravala, Gujarat. It is located under the shade of a huge sal tree. A devotee of Mahadeva worshipped the deity daily to become rich. Finally, his prayer was fulfilled, and he became extraordinarily rich through a series of miraculous incidents. The devotee was immensely happy. He wanted to do something great as his wish was granted. As the shrine of the deity was very small, he planned to build a grand temple of bricks and stone with beautiful paintings. So, he instructed the builders to go ahead with the construction of the temple.

When the builders approached him about cutting the sal tree as it was causing obstruction, he immediately accepted their idea. Accordingly, a team of masons and labourers arranged for a wood cutter to cut the tree the next day. But the wealthy man did not have a peaceful sleep that night. Bhimanatha Mahadeva appeared before him in his dream and expressed his unhappiness at the idea of cutting the sal tree for building a temple as the sal tree was not only home for him but also for many other gods. The rich man repented his mistake and promised not to disturb the tree. Therefore, the idea of building a temple by cutting the sal tree was dropped. Even now, the small shrine stands under the sal tree, and devotees worship Bhimanatha Mahadeva and offer flowers to the sal tree.

Usage

The dry leaves of the sal tree are used to produce leaf plates in northern and eastern India. Fresh leaves are used to serve readymade *paan* (betel nut preparations) and small snacks such as boiled black gram, etc. The used leaves/plates are eaten by goats and other cattle. Thus, the tree has protected northern India from plastic menace to a great extent. In Nepal, the leaves of the tree are used to serve rice and curry. The aromatic resin obtained from the tree is used to burn as incense and to caulk boats and ships. Its fruit oil is used to light lamps and adulterate ghee in north India. The oil extracted from its seeds is used to cook after refining and as a substitute for cocoa butter in making chocolates. Sal is a major source of hardwood timber in India. The wood finds applications in hydraulic engineering, ships, railway cars, poles, railway sleepers, posts, as well as for interior finishing purposes like

Pristine *Shorea robusta* flowers
Shot by Delonix, https://tinyurl.com/2vdyssrn, licensed under CC BY-SA 4.0

window frames and floors.

The resin is used to treat dysentery, gonorrhoea, boils and toothache. The leaf juice is used to treat dysentery. The leaves are heated and used as a poultice on parts of the body that are swollen. It is applied to treat dysentery in children. The oil obtained from the seeds is used to treat skin diseases.

Cultivation Practices

The seeds are soaked in water for 12 hours before sowing. The pre-treated seeds are sown in mother beds and covered with a thin layer of sand or sawdust. Germination of fresh seeds is usually good. When the seedlings are about 6 cm tall, they are transplanted into containers; 40–45 cm tall saplings are ready for planting. This is suitable for intercropping also. In Assam, regeneration of sal is practised in combination with crops such as upland rice, maize, sesame and mustard. Successful plantations of sal mixed with teak have yielded good results.

Trumpet Flower (Stereospermum suaveolens)

Trumpet Flower

Family: Bignoniaceae

The trumpet flower, scientifically known as *Stereospermum suaveolens* (Roxb.) DC., belongs to the Bignoniaceae family. This is one among the *Dashamoola* group of herbs (group of ten roots). Thiru Padiri Puliyur, where the famous temple of Lord Shiva is located in Tamil Nadu, is named after this sacred tree (*padiri* is its Tamil name). This is called trumpet flower as the flower of the tree has the shape of a trumpet. This is said to possess medical properties that can cure cancer.

The trumpet flower is a large tree growing in deciduous forest; it grows up to a height of 25 m with a spreading crown. The tree flowers in May–June. The fragrant and trumpet-shaped flowers are dark purple in colour. Fruiting occurs in December–January.

The trade name of this tree is padiri. Its common English names are trumpet flower, bignonia or yellow snake. This is also called *parul* in Assamese ; parul in Bengali; *padal* in Gujarati; *padhal* and *podal* in Hindi; *billa* and *pudika* in Kannada; *kariyam* and padiri in Malayalam; padal in Marathi; *boro* and *patulee* in Odia; padal in Punjabi; *paatali, patali, paatala* and *patala* in Sanskrit; padiri in Tamil; and padiri, *kalagoru* and *kaligottu* in Telugu.

Stereospermum suaveolens flowers are said to spread cheer in Karnataka.
Shot by Delonix, https://tinyurl.com/2s3fd72u, licensed under CC BY-SA 3.0

Habitat and Distribution

The patala tree is a large deciduous tree. This tree generally grows in deciduous forests. This species is distributed in India, Myanmar, Sri Lanka Cambodia, Laos, Myanmar, Thailand, Vietnam and Malaysia. This is found in tropical Himalayas, Assam and Meghalaya as well as in the moist deciduous forests of the Western Ghats.

Religious Significance

According to Shiva Purana, patala is one of the 11 flowers with which Lord Shiva is worshipped. This is a tree of the

Panchavati forest where Lord Rama stayed during his forest exile. This is a tree of Pampa Sarovar, which he visited during his forest exile. This tree is associated with Simha (Leo) zodiac as per Hindu mythology.

In Buddhism and Jainism, it is said that Bodhisatva Vipaasi and Tirthankara Vasupujya, respectively, attained enlightenment under a patala tree. Tamil saint-poet Thirunavukkarasar has discussed this tree in Thevaram. It is worshipped as sacred in the temples of Lord Shiva built at Thiru Padiri Puliyur, Thiruvalithayam, Thiruavinasi and Thiruvarur of Tamil Nadu. The patala tree is also considered sacred in the temples of Lord Vishnu located in Thiru Adhanur and Thiru Nagai in Tamil Nadu.

Mythological Significance

According to a tale in Hari Vamsa, King Himavant and his wife Mena were blessed with three daughters. The eldest was called Aparna, whose name meant 'without any leaf'. The younger daughters were known as Eka-parna and Eka-patali, both names meaning one leaf. They were called these special names as they practised extraordinary abstinence and austerities in order to marry Lord Mahadeva. While the two younger sisters managed to live on only one patala leaf, the eldest managed without any leaf at all. Eka-parna performed penances under a banyan tree for 200 years. Eka-patali performed penances for 2,000 years under the wood of the wild Himalayan cherry tree. This made their mother unhappy, and she worried about the health of her daughter. So, in a distressed mood, Mena cried out to her daughter Aparna saying, '*U-ma*', which means 'Oh-don't'. From that time, Aparna, the eldest daughter came to be known as Uma. As Aparna did extraordinary abstinence and austerities in order to marry Lord Mahadeva, pleased with her penance, Lord Mahadeva accepted Aparna as his consort. Thus, the patala leaf on which Aparna's two sisters subsisted became closely associated with Lord Shiva and the patala tree became sacred.

Usage

The patala leaves are used as fodder for cattle. The wood is used to make furniture, tea boxes, in construction, etc. It can be planted along avenues in towns and cities. It filters dust besides providing shade. As the tree has good medicinal properties, it is advisable to plant the tree on the banks of ponds, lakes and in wastelands. This tree can be grown in the premises of big buildings especially in coastal towns.

The leaves are useful in relieving burning sensation and pain. The flowers are useful in blood detoxification and is good for the heart. The fruits are used to treat hiccups, diarrhoea, burning sensation, chest injuries and male and female infertility problems. The root and root bark are used to treat inflammation, asthma, bronchitis, pain, neurological disorders, haemorrhoids, constipation, snake bite and scorpion bite and gastric ulcers.

Cultivation Practices

The seeds are sown in the nursery bed. Germination starts after two weeks. Seedlings with four leaves are transplanted into containers. One-year-old seedlings can be planted in the field with a spacing of 6 m × 6 m. Watering is necessary for better establishment of the trees.

Jamun Tree (*Syzygium cumini*)

Jamun

Family: Myrtaceae

The jamun, scientifically known as *Syzygium cumini* (L.) Skeels belongs to the family Myrtaceae. This is also called *Syzygium jambolanum* DC or *Eugenia jambolana* Lam. The name '*Eugenia*' is derived from Eugene, Prince of Savoy, a prominent botany patron in the seventeenth century. '*Syzygium*' is derived from the Greek word '*suzogos*,' meaning paired. '*Jambolana*' is from the East Indies* word '*jambos*' or rose apple which finds its name in Hindi as jambu and then jamun. This tree has significant religious, cultural and medicinal values.

The jamun is a large, evergreen tree growing to a height of 30 m and can live for more than 100 years. As the dense foliage provides good shade, this is grown for its ornamental value also. The tree flowers in February–May and fruiting occurs in June–August. The oblong to ovoid fruit is pink when unripe and changes into purplish black when ripe.

This is commonly known as jamun, java plum, black plum, Indian cherry, jambu or Indian blackberry. This has various local names such as *kaljam* in Bengali; jamboo in Gujarati; jamun and *phalinda* in Hindi; *nerali* in Kannada; *naval* in Malayalam; *jambhul* in Marathi; jambu and *phalendra* in Sanskrit; *naval* in Tamil; and *neraelu* in Telugu.

---

*East Indies refers to a group of islands in the Indian and Pacific oceans between Asia and Australia.

Habitat and Distribution

Jamun is an evergreen tropical tree. This tree is found growing in all forests, both in plains and hills up to 1,800 m. This is mostly planted along the roadsides and in gardens for shade and fruits. This is native to the Indian subcontinent and the regions of Southeast Asia, China and Australia. As this tree is spread overseas by emigrants, it is commonly found in tropical countries that were former British colonies. This tree was also introduced in Florida in 1911, and is commonly found growing in Suriname, Guyana and Trinidad and Tobago. This was introduced to Brazil from India during Portuguese colonization.

Cultural Significance

Jamun leaves are used to decorate marriage pandals in Maharashtra. The story of Jambulaakhyan from the Mahabharata is related to jamun fruit. A branch of the jamun tree is worshipped while beginning wedding preparations among Hindus in Andhra Pradesh and the same is planted in the place where the pandal will be erected. In Indian culture, beautiful eyes are compared to the jamun fruit. The leaves of this tree are made into garlands and hung over the entrance of houses to ensure perpetuity and continuity and a stable marriage. The jamun trees are found commonly in the states of Tamil Nadu, Kerala and Karnataka.

In Tamil Nadu state, jamun is worshipped as a sacred tree in 11 temples of Shiva, Murugan, Vishnu and Ayyanar. The gods of seven Shiva temples have been named after this tree in Tamil Nadu. About 40 villages in Tamil Nadu and 70 villages in Andhra Pradesh, Assam, Bihar, Gujarat, Karnataka, Kerala, Madhya Pradesh, Maharashtra and Rajasthan and Andaman and Nicobar Islands have been named after this tree, with 42 villages in Gujarat alone. Jamun is highly praised in ancient Tamil literature by different poets. Both men and women are named after this tree in Tamil Nadu.

Mythological Significance

In Indian mythology, the jamun tree is closely associated with the star Rohini, which holds significance in the almanac. The Mahabharata beautifully compares the colour of Lord Krishna's body to the jamun fruit, highlighting its unique hue. This tree was widely known as Jambavam and had a widespread distribution throughout ancient India. Historical records indicate that the tree was first noticed south of Mahameru and was regarded as one of the most majestic trees (Mahavriksha) on Earth. Legend narrates the tale of Goddess Jamboodini, who resided for a prolonged period on the banks of the river Jamboo, taking great delight in the delectable jamun fruits. Her unwavering devotion drew worship from all devas, asuras and nagas who sought salvation. Interestingly, ancient mining experts believed that the plentiful presence of jamun trees in an area was an indicator of potential gold mines in the vicinity. Following this belief, a gold mine was eventually discovered on the bank of the river Jamboo, where miners struck high-quality gold, lending a fascinating touch to the connection between the jamun tree and the quest for precious treasures.

There is an interesting mythological story in ancient Tamil Literature. The famous Tamil poetess Avvaiyar was once sitting under a jamun tree. Since she had written a lot of poems in Tamil, she was egoistic. Lord Muruga, the popular Tamil god, wanted to deflate her ego. So, he took the form of a shepherd and sat on the tree. He asked Avvaiyar, 'Grandma, you look tired. Do you want some naval fruits?' When she answered yes, he asked, 'Do you want *sutta pazham* or *sudaatha pazham*?' (The word 'sutta' has two meanings in Tamil: cooked and hot.) Avvaiyar, thinking the shepherd was illiterate, told him to provide sudaatha pazham (fruit that is not roasted or hot). She was filled with the feeling of being very knowledgeable. When the boy shook the tree, the fruits fell all over the ground. Avvaiyar collected the fruits and started blowing on them to remove the sand that was stuck to the fruits. At that time, the shepherd boy exclaimed, 'Is the fruit hot?' The act of blowing away the sand on the fruit was like blowing air to cool something, making it appear that the fruit was hot. On hearing the clever words of the boy, Avvaiyar suddenly had a realization. She thought that the shepherd boy was illiterate, but he taught her a lesson. She realized that no one should be neglected and started singing a song eloquently. She knew that this would be the act of someone divine and requested the boy to reveal his real persona. The shepherd revealed who he was, and there was Lord Muruga, standing in front of her. Avvaiyar felt immensely happy and paid obeisance to him. It is believed that this incident took place in Pazhamudir Cholai, near Azhagar Kovil, Madurai, one of the six abodes of Lord Muruga in Tamil Nadu. She was inspired towards further learning and writing by this incident. Avvaiyar's poems meant for young ones are still widely read all over Tamil Nadu.

Jamun fruits at various stage of maturity
Shot by Nikitakamka, https://tinyurl.com/2e3k6dsw, licensed under CC BY-SA 4.0

Jamun, Fruit of the Gods: According to belief, during his 14-year exile from Ayodhya, Lord Rama sustained himself on the jamun fruit in the forest. Hindus consider jamun as a divine fruit, particularly in Gujarat, where it is referred to as jamboo. Lord Megha, the god of the clouds, is said to have descended on Earth in the form of a jamun tree, and that is why the colour of the fruit is dark and stormy as that of the fierce monsoon clouds. The ancient Puranas explain the splitting of the cosmos into seven island continents with Jambudvipa, the land of the jambu trees, at the centre of the cosmos. These trees are described to be as large as elephants in the Vishnu Purana, and when the rotten fruit fell on the mountainous land, a river was formed from their rich purple juice.

Usage

The leaves are used as fodder for livestock because of the nutritional value. The fruits are made into jams, sherbet, jelly, juice, puddings, etc. A coffee-like beverage is prepared from the dried and ground seeds. The brown dye obtained from the bark is used in colouring and preserving fishnet. The branches are used to whiten the teeth. As the wood is water resistant, it is used in railway sleepers and for installing motors in wells. The wood is used for making furniture, houses and boats, agricultural implements, tool handles, cart wheels, etc. In addition, it serves as a material for constructing bridges and crafting musical instruments, particularly guitars. The jamun tree provides good fuel too. The bark is used for tanning. It can be grown as a hedge or as a windbreak. This can also be inter-planted with crops like banana, coffee and cocoa as a shade provider. Its flowers attract bees, and they yield quality honey.

The fruits and the seeds of the jamun tree are used to treat diabetes. The seeds and the bark are used to cure dysentery and diabetes. The juice obtained from the bark is used to treat wounds and enlargement of the spleen. An infusion of the bark is used to treat irregular menstruation, diarrhoea, dysentery and children's thrush. The bark can be used as a gargle to strengthen gums and to treat mouth ulcers. The fruits are used to treat colic and diarrhoea. An infusion of the leaves can be used to treat diabetes and diarrhoea. The roots are used to treat epilepsy.

Cultivation Practices

Freshly collected seeds are to be sown in mother beds. A kilogram may have 1,100–1,300 seeds. Germination may start after fourteen days and completes by 125 days. At the initial stage, the seedlings may require sufficient moisture and shade. Seedlings with four leaves are pricked into containers; 60-cm-tall seedlings are ready for planting, and 6 m × 6 m spacing can be followed. Seed-origin trees may start yielding only after 8–10 years. Quality trees produced through vegetative propagation may yield after five years. This tree can tolerate drought. It is a good coppicer. It is a versatile tree that can grow on shallow and rocky soil too if the rainfall is sufficient.

Tamarind Tree (*Tamarindus indica*)

Tamarind

Family: Caesalpiniaceae

Tamarind, scientifically known as *Tamarindus indica* L., belongs to the Caesalpiniaceae family. The name 'tamarind' is derived from the Persian *Tamar-i-Hind*, meaning Indian date, from the date-like appearance of the dried pulp. The specific name '*indica*' refers to the Indian origin of the tree. The Sanskrit word '*amlika*' means sour taste. Presently, India is the largest producer of tamarind. The edible pulp of the pod-like fruit produced by this tree is used in cuisines all over the world. The pulp is also used in traditional medicine and for polishing metal objects.

Tamarind is a large, evergreen tree, mostly planted along roadsides for its dense shade and the pulp of its fruits. This is a long-lived tree growing to a height of 12–18 m. The leaflets close at night. The red-and-yellow-coloured flowers appear in April–June. Fruiting occurs in October–December. The fruit with the fleshy, juicy and acidulous pulp is mature when it becomes brown or reddish brown. The fruit tastes sweet and sour.

The trade name of this tree is tamarind. It is called *amli* and *tentul* in Bengali; amli and *imli* in Hindi; *hunase* in Kannada; *puli* in Malayalam; *mange* in Manipuri; amli and *chinch* in Marathi; amlika in Sanskrit; puli in Tamil; and *chinta* in Telugu.

Habitat and Distribution

Since it has been cultivated in India from time immemorial, it is sometimes reported as native to the Indian subcontinent. However, tamarind is indigenous to tropical Africa. As a large, evergreen tree, it is cultivated around the world in tropical and subtropical zones. It is found growing wild in Sudan, Cameroon, Nigeria, Zambia, Tanzania, as well as in Oman, on the sea-facing slopes of mountains. It is distributed throughout the tropical region, from Africa to South Asia, northern Australia, Southeast Asia, Taiwan and China. In the sixteenth century, tamarind was introduced in Mexico and South America. As this plays a major role in the cuisines of the Indian subcontinent, Southeast Asia and Mexico, it is consumed widely.

Sacredness

Tamarind is considered sacred by Africans. The Burmese believe that the rain god resides under the tamarind tree. It is a common practice in Malaya to feed infants with a concoction made of tamarind pulp and coconut milk. The bark of the tree is believed to be the source of wisdom. The tamarind tree is considered sacred in about 12 temples in Tamil Nadu which are meant for Shiva, Vishnu, Murugan and Ayyanar. About 130 villages in Tamil Nadu and around 15 villages in states like Andhra Pradesh, Assam and Kerala are named after this tree. Many puzzles and numerous proverbs associated with the tamarind tree have been developed in Tamil. This tree has special names in Tamil literature too.

Mythological Significance

Tamarind is also known as *tintrini* in Sanskrit. There is an interesting story from the Birhor tribe, living in the Indian state of Jharkhand, associated with the tree. During their exile of 14 years, Rama, Lakshmana and Sita reached a forest, where a lot of tintrini trees were growing. In those days, the tree had large and well-developed leaves. The trio made a hut under the tree and had a comfortable stay, well-protected from rain and intense heat and cold. Rama felt that they were supposed to suffer privations and inconveniences while in exile. So, he ordered Lakshmana to shoot at the leaves and split them. Accordingly, Lakshmana shot at the leaves, and, since then, the leaves have been finely divided.

A Sambalpuri legend of Odisha also describes why the leaves of the tamarind tree are so small. Long ago, when both gods and asuras ruled over the Earth, Bhasmasura was the chief of the asura or demon army. He challenged Mahadeva, that is, Shiva, to a duel. The decision was made that the victorious one would become the ruler of the Earth. The two fought, and Bhasmasura was wounded badly, so he ran for his life. He fled through the forest and hid himself in a tamarind tree with huge spreading branches and giant leaves. Shiva searched for the demon and, as he passed under the tree, Bhasmasura shook nervously and the leaves rustled. Shiva looked up and knew that the asura had been found, but could not see him. He tried his best to get him, but the giant leaves hid Bhasmasura well. Shiva lost his patience. With a roar of rage, he opened his third eye and turned each giant leaf into small leaves. Finally, Shiva found Bhasmasura and killed him. It is believed that the leaves of the tamarind have been small since then.

There is an interesting Odia tribal story about this tree too. Bimma, a tribal man, planted a plantain tree with large leaves. Another tribal man named Ramma was jealous of Bimma. He planted a tamarind tree that had large leaves in those days. Bimma did not like this. So, he sent a parrot to break the leaves of the tamarind tree into shreds. The parrot did this, and, since then, the leaves have remained small.

In Hindu mythology, tamarind has become popular because of its association with Usha, the adopted daughter of Lord Shiva and Goddess Parvathi. One day, when Shiva was returning after his bath, he saw his daughter Usha playing with his minor son Ganesha. Shiva had been in a bad mood and was enraged further by both Usha and Ganesha for ignoring his presence. He cut off his son's head. On seeing that, Parvathi lamented and prayed to Shiva to bring Ganesha back to life. So, at the request of Parvathi, Shiva replaced the severed head of his son with that of an elephant and revived the child. Usha, who happened to see the incident, was frightened and hid herself in a barrel of salt to evade the wrath of Shiva.

Parvathi became angry with Usha for not having looked after Ganesha properly and cursed her to be born on earth as the daughter of the demon Banasura in Tezpur, Assam. Usha pleaded with Parvathi to forgive her. Listening to her earnest prayers, Parvathi granted her the boon that in Usha's memory, no salt would be taken in the month of Chaitra, but instead, the juice of the tamarind fruit would be used to season food. Usha married Aniruddha, the grandson of Krishna, and lived with him in Dwaraka. Thus, Usha is remembered when eating meals without salt in the month of Chaitra. Generally, the fruit or flowers of the tamarind tree are not used on any auspicious occasion as they have a sour taste, and there is a

Bitter sweet: Tamarind tree
Shot by Thamizhpparithi Maari, https://tinyurl.com/mth8tt5m, licensed under CC BY-SA 3.0

common belief that any occasion where tamarind is offered may not yield fruitful results.

Common folklore suggests that the tamarind tree is the home of spirits that do not allow anything under the tree to survive. For this reason, travellers are advised not to sleep under the tree.

A famous tamarind tree in India is in Gwalior, growing over the tomb of Emperor Akbar's musician Tansen. Legend says that all classical singers should eat some leaves of this tree to have a voice as sweet as Tansen's.

Usage

The leaves are used as fodder for livestock. Tender leaves are cooked and eaten. The flowers also are cooked and consumed. Unripe fruits are used for making chutney. Though the pulp of the young fruit is sour, it is used in preparation of savoury dishes. The pulp of the tamarind fruit is edible. The ripe fruit becomes sweet and is more palatable. The fruit paste is used to add flavour to chutneys, curries, syrups, etc. The sweet chutney prepared out of tamarind fruit pulp is famous in India and Pakistan. The fruit pulp is considered the main ingredient of South Indian cuisine. Across the Middle East, the Philippines and Indonesia, the tamarind fruit is used for making delicious dishes. Seeds are used in making jams, jellies and confectionary. The seed oil obtained from the kernel can be used in making paint and varnish. The powder of the kernel is used in textile and jute processing, and in making industrial gums and adhesives. Wood is used for making furniture, carvings, oil presses, turnery, etc. The fruit pulp is used for polishing idols, lamps and utensils made up of copper, brass and bronze.

The leaves, flowers and pulp in different combinations are used to treat pain in swollen joints. Tamarind juice is used to treat bile disorders, sore throats and sunstroke as well as to control cholesterol levels. Eye drops obtained from tamarind seeds are used to treat dry eye syndrome. Generally, consumption of tamarind helps to reduce heart-related problems. It helps in losing overweight. Its pulp also improves digestion and prevents ulcers.

Cultivation Practices

Propagation through seed is a common practice. However, seed-origin trees may take about 15–20 years for economic yield. Trees developed through vegetative propagation are preferred as their yield starts after 3–4 years when provided with optimum growing conditions. Grafting, budding and air layering methods are followed to produce desirable cultivars. Pits of 1 m × 1 m × 1 m size are followed. The spacing may vary from 8 m × 8 m to 10 × 10 m depending on the soil type. Intercropping is initially entertained. Crops like cowpea, horse gram, drumstick, tomato, chilly, etc., can be planted during the initial period of 4–5 years to check soil erosion and improve soil health. Saplings are to be provided with support of bamboo sticks and irrigation is to be done during the summer months up to 3–4 years. Fruits are harvested in January–April. A well-managed tree may yield about 200 kg of ripe pods. The pulp collected after removal of the shell, seeds and the fibrous material is dried in the sun and can be stored up to 6–12 months.

Arjuna Tree (*Terminalia arjuna*)

Arjuna

Family: Combretaceae

Arjuna, scientifically known as *Terminalia arjuna* (Roxb.) Wight & Arn., belongs to the Combretaceae family. This is one of the trees of the genus Terminalia. The name '*Terminalia*' is derived from Latin '*terminus*' or '*terminalis*' meaning 'ending', referring to the flowers being crowded together at the ends of the branches. The specific name '*arjuna*' occurs in the Rig Veda and Atharva Veda, and means 'white' or 'bright', denoting the creamy-white flowers and the shining quality of the bark. The tree is also known as *kakubha* in Sanskrit, meaning 'beauty' and 'fascination'. The arjuna tree has been used for at least 3,000 years in treating heart disease and, because of this, the tree has the nickname guardian of the heart.

The arjuna is a large tree usually with buttressed trunk growing to a height of about 20 m. Generally, the tree forms a wide canopy at the crown with drooping branches. The tree exhibits smooth and grey bark. Pale yellow and honey-scented flowers appear in April–May and the woody fruit with five wings appears in November–January.

The common English name for this tree is arjun. It is called arjun in Assamese; arjuna and arjun in Hindi; *neer maruthu, nirmathi* and *aathumaruthu* in Kannada; *aathumaruthu, nirmaruthu, neer marudhu* and *vellamathi* in Malayalam; *maiyokpha* in Manipuri; *kakubha* and arjuna in Sanskrit; and *kula maruthu, vellai maruthu* and *maruthu* in Tamil. It is also called *partha* (synonymous with Arjuna of the Mahabharata), *dhaval* (because of its greenish white bark), *kukumbha* (huge tree) and *nathisarj* (distributed in the river beds).

Habitat and Distribution

The arjuna tree is commonly found growing on stream banks in moist deciduous forests. Outside of forests, this tree is found on the banks of rivers and near dry riverbeds in North and South India. A native of the Indian subcontinent, this is also found in Bangladesh, Myanmar and Sri Lanka.

Dear Old Friend of a Former Indian President: A former President of India, the late Dr A.P.J. Abdul Kalam, had a dear old friend who shared his official home at 10, Rajaji Marg in New Delhi. Any guesses who that friend was? It was none other than a 100-year-old arjuna tree. The late president was very fond of this tree and spent time with it almost daily. He would observe the 300-kg beehive hanging from its branch and the bevy of birds, such as cuckoos, mynas, sparrows, crows, etc., for whom the tree provided food and shelter. Dr Kalam said that the tree was like his parents; his father was over a 100 and his mother was older than 90 when they passed away. He had developed great affection for the tree and felt that it was a living testament to life itself and disclosed many things about nature to him.

Mythological Significance

In the Ashtanga Hridayam and in many ancient Indian Vedas, it was known for treating heart diseases for thousands of years. The arjuna was introduced into Siddha by the great Tamil saint Agastiya. Maharishi Vagbhata, one of the most influential classical writers of Ayurveda, introduced it into Ayurveda medical system. Vagbhata discussed the use of this tree in treating wounds, haemorrhages and ulcers.

Religious Siginificance

There is mention of the arjuna tree in the Bala Kanda of the Ramayana as growing in Malada and Karusha (today's Datia district of Madhya Pradesh). It is said that this tree is named after Arjuna, the hero of the Mahabharata. However, this appears to be incorrect, as the name 'arjuna' for this tree is found in the Rig Veda and Atharva Veda, both of which are much older than the Mahabharata.

Arjuna Veervriksha: Arjuna, also known as *indradru*, derives its name from 'huge tree', symbolizing its strength and stability. People often refer to this tree as *veervriksha* (the soldier tree) due to its resilient nature. In Hindu mythology, the arjuna tree is linked to the star Swathi, and it is believed that those born under this star may share similar attributes. For individuals who place faith in Vedic astrology and are born under the Swathi star, planting and nurturing an arjuna tree is advised. This practice is believed to bring about peace, prosperity, and protection from negative influences, making it a significant aspect of their spiritual journey.

In Theravada Buddhism, arjuna is believed to be the tree under which the tenth Buddha, known as Anomadassi Buddha, attained enlightenment.

Arjuna is worshipped as sacred in about 15 temples in Tamil Nadu. Lord Shiva has been named after this tree in two temples here. About 65 villages in Tamil Nadu and eight in Kerala have been named after this tree in the state. This tree has been portrayed by many poets like Nakkerar, Baranar, Kundriyanar, Neelakesi, etc., in Tamil literature. Both men and women in Tamil Nadu have been named after this tree. The popular saint-poet Thirugnanasambandar discussed the arjuna tree in Thevaram.

There is mention of the arjuna tree in the Bhagavatam, which describes the life story of Lord Krishna. The story illustrates how infant Krishna delivered two gods from a curse because of which they had been born as arjuna trees on Earth. Little Krishna was very mischievous in Gokulam and, unable to manage the naughty Krishna, his mother Yashodha tied him up with a rope to a large wooden mortar in which buttermilk was churned. The infant was displeased because of this. He could not sit quietly in one place. A wooden mortar was nothing for the divine child, so he dragged the mortar and slowly came out of the house. Noticing two large arjuna trees outside their house, he decided to pass through the gap between the trees. In the process, the wooden mortar got struck between the trees.

When little Krishna tried to pull the mortar, the two trees were uprooted and fell on the ground. The very next moment, two heavenly beings appeared from the trunks and fell at Krishna's feet, bowing their heads. They offered their prayers and started explaining what had happened to them. They were

The roots of the *Terminalia arjuna* tree at the Hogenakkal Falls in Dharmapuri district, Tamil Nadu
Shot by Emöke Dénes, https://tinyurl.com/47ffdka6. Licensed under CC BY-SA 4.0

Nalakuvara and Manigriva, the sons of Kubera, the treasurer of the gods. As they were rich and idle, they had become accustomed to women and wine. Once, when they were so occupied, the great sage Narada happened to pass by. As they had consumed too much alcohol and were in the company of women, they failed to show respect to the sage. Enraged by their misbehaviour, Narada became angry and cursed them to become two arjuna trees in Gokulam. Learning this, the wives of Nalakuvara and Manigriva rushed to the sage and pleaded with him to take back the curse. Narada told them that a curse once given could not be taken back and their husbands would be released by Lord Vishnu himself when he took the incarnation of Krishna. Now, as the prophecy was fulfilled, Nalakuvara and Manigriva thanked Lord Krishna and left for their heavenly abode.

In Hindu mythlology, arjuna is supposed to be Sita's favourite tree. The leaves and flowers of this tree are offered to Lord Vishnu and Lord Ganapathi on religious occasions.

Usage

A decoction of the bark is mixed with milk and used as a beverage. The wood is used for agricultural implements, building carts, boats and mine props. The bark is used for tanning. Arjuna leaves are eaten by the moth that produces tussar silk, a wild silk of commercial importance. Juice from the leaves is used to treat earache. The bark is used to treat cardiac problems, blood pressure and to reduce blood cholesterol level. The bark is taken internally to treat a range of heart ailments and proved to work best when the blood supply to the heart is poor. It is used to maintain a steady heartbeat. The great Ayurvedic masters of India recognized the excellent therapeutic potential and effectively used this for managing heart problems. This tree was considered as a saviour from fatal diseases like heart attack and stroke.

Cultivation Practices

After drying the fruits in sunlight, they are stored for a period of 6–12 months. To prepare the seeds for sowing, they are pretreated by soaking in water for 48 hours. Germination takes place in 12–50 days; 8–9-month-old seedlings are optimum for transplanting in the field. Spacing of 6 m × 6 m can be followed. Watering is required initially for early establishment of the trees. The initial growth may be fast. Support has to be provided for the younger trees.

Ber/Jujub Tree (*Ziziphus jujuba*)

Ber or Jujub

Family: Rhamnaceae

Ber or jujub, scientifically known as *Ziziphus jujuba* (L.) Gaertn., belongs to the Rhamnaceae family. The word '*Ziziphus*' is derived from the Arabic '*zizouf*', meaning a nut-bearing lotus. '*Zizyphon*' is the Greek word for jujube, an edible plum-like fruit. The Latin word '*Zizyphwn*' also has the same meaning. This is also known as *Ziziphus mauritiana* Lamk. *Ziziphus jujuba* has been listed as a threatened species by the International Union for Conservation of Nature (IUCN)..

The ber tree is generally a thorny, deciduous tree. Sometimes, this grows as a shrub. This can grow up to 10 m tall. The tree usually spreads through root suckers. This may be evergreen or leafless for several weeks in hot summer. The tree flowers in September–November and fruiting occurs in December–February. The fleshy fruits are orange or red in colour and are edible.

The English names for this tree are Chinese date, Chinese fig or jujube. Its trade name is jujub. This is also known as *kul* in Bengali; ber in Hindi; *elachi* in Kannada; *cherumali* and *elantha* in Malayalam; *bor* in Marathi; *badara* and *badari* in Sanskrit; *ilanthai* in Tamil; and *reghu* in Telugu.

Habitat and Distribution

The ber tree is found in dry districts and dry deciduous forests. This is also cultivated in and around villages and grows naturally on wastelands. This species also grows in dry gravelly or stony slopes of hills.

This species is native to the region spanning Yunnan Province in southern China, Afghanistan, Malaysia and Queensland in Australia. The ber tree was domesticated in South Asia around 9000 BCE. Wild trees are found in India up to an elevation of 1,600 m. It is cultivated and grown commercially in India up to 1,000 m. This species has been spread over Hawaii, the West Indies, the Bahamas, Colombia, Venezuela, Guatemala and southern Florida. It is almost naturalized in Barbados, Jamaica and Puerto Rico. This has flourished in Israel after its introduction from Malaysia in 1939.

Historical Significance

The ber tree has been described in the ancient Puranic stories, Brahmanam, Yajur Veda and medical books. Ancient Sanskrit scholars like Kautilya, Panini, Patanjali and Valmiki also wrote about the ber tree.

Badrinath Named after Ber Tree: Badrinath, the sacred pilgrimage centre of the Hindus, located on the western bank of the Alaknanda at the foot of the Himalayas, was said to have had groves of ber trees once upon a time. The hermits and their disciples ate the fruits of this tree. As plenty of ber (badari) trees were available then, the place was called Badrika. Subsequently, the name of the place is changed to the present name, Badrinath.

∼

The ber tree has been discussed in folklore in North India, especially Punjab. As the presence of the ber tree within the house is believed to make the residents quarrel, it is considered unlucky to plant it within the premises of the house. The Sikhs hold great reverence for the Dukhbhanjani, also known as the sorrow-removing tree, which grows inside the Golden Temple in Amritsar. This tree is associated with Baba Buda, the chief priest of the Golden Temple and the disciple of Guru Nanak. This tree is said to be about 400 years old.

Once, a Muslim contractor presented a hybrid variety of the fruit to Raja Raghoji Bhonsale II of Ahmadnagar. The contractor was suitably awarded with a royal gift by the Raja for his act of kindness. It is said that after that incident, the cultivation of this tree was started in this region.

The thornless ber tree found in Jabrabad village of Amaredi district in Gujarat is also said to be about 400 years old. It is said that Arab traders had given two thornless saplings to Rajabai Alabai Katsam, a blacksmith who worked under them. While one died, the other one survived; it is considered to be this tree. This has grown to a height of 15 m and gives an annual yield of 600 kg fruits. At the same time, this tree is not attacked by any pest or insect.

It is believed that the fruits had been dispersed by pilgrims from Badrinath to other areas over a period of time. In ancient times, the presence of the ber tree was taken as the indicator of a groundwater source. If the ber tree was found on an anthill, it was believed that water would be available at a depth of fifteen feet.

The ber tree is worshipped as a sacred tree in the temples of Lord Shiva located in Thirukeelvelur, Thirunanaa and Thiruomampuliyur of Tamil Nadu state. This tree is discussed by the great saint-poet Thirunavukkarasar in Thevaram.

Mythological Significance

The Ramayana describes the sturdiness of the ber tree. During Rama's exile, Sita disappeared suddenly. Rama and Lakshmana were shocked by her disappearance. They started searching for her anxiously, but did not know in which direction to proceed. At that time, they heard the call of a shabby, ill-kempt, odd-looking ber tree. The tree told them that it saw Sita being carried away. The tree further added that when it tried to stop her by pulling at her dress, it could only tear her garment with its weak branches and a piece of her dress was clinging to its thorns. After informing Rama, the tree drooped in disgrace. Rama was pleased by the useful information given by the tree and blessed it. He told the tree that it would attain immortality and come back to life from a single root, even if it was hacked down to its roots by men.

In the Tamil epic Kamba Ramayana, the sacredness of the ber tree has been discussed in detail. There was a gandharva king by name Chitravacha. He had a daughter, Malini. She was not faithful to her husband, Vitihotra. So, she was cursed to be born in a tribe of forest dwellers. The tears shed by Malini moved her husband. He became merciful towards his wife and told her that Lord Vishnu as Rama would remove her curse. Malini took rebirth as Shabari near Sage Matanga's hermitage in the forest. She served Rama's devotees and waited for the arrival of Rama. During their search for Sita, Rama and Lakshmana came across her hut. Seeing them, Shabari was pleased and rushed inside the house to fetch something to offer them. But there was nothing available except a few fruits

Bowl of jujube fruit
Shot by Srinayan, https://tinyurl.com/5ezvs22e, licensed under CC BY 3.0

of the ber tree that grew near the hut. Shabari wanted Rama to have sweet berries. So, she bit each fruit and offered only the sweet ones to the brothers. She discarded the sour ones.

Rama ate the fruits given to him and understood the love and devotion which had made the illiterate woman taste the fruits. But the meticulous Lakshmana threw away the bitten fruits. It is believed that the life-saving herb Sanjivani grew out of the fruit thrown by him and, later, this herb saved him while he lay dying. Pleased with the offerings of the sweet berries, Rama blessed Shabari for her devotion. She was then transformed into Malini, the gandharva woman, and her husband, Vitihotra, appeared by her side. After worshipping Lord Rama, he took his wife away to the city of gandharvas in the sky.

The ber tree has been revered as sacred both in the Hindu epic and in a legend related to Sikhism.

Ber, Sorrow-Removing Tree: A Punjabi legend describes how the ber tree acted as a sorrow remover. There was a nobleman named Duli Chand in a town called Patti. He had five daughters. Out of the five, four were married, but the youngest, Bibi Rajni, was unmarried. He and his wife prayed for years to have a son. As they were not blessed with a son, he was very disappointed. One day, all five sisters went out on a picnic. They noticed some ascetics reciting devotional songs. The youngest daughter was so moved by the hermits that she removed her jewels and distributed them to the ascetics. The sisters then returned home. On their return, the father noticed the youngest one with bare arms and neck. He called his daughters and asked each one of them, 'Who protects and gives you food, clothes and jewels?' The four elder daughters replied that it was their father. But the youngest daughter said that it was god who protects and gives her everything. Enraged by her answer, the father got her married to a person suffering from leprosy. He told his youngest daughter that he would see how god would help them.

The newly-wed couple were sent out of the house. Bibi Rajni took her husband to different villages and managed to survive with whatever food they got through begging. She visited many temples along with her husband. Then they came to Amritsar. Bibi Rajni helped her husband sit under a ber tree on the banks of a pond and went begging. Sitting under the tree, her husband saw the miracle of a jet-black crow diving into the water of the nearby pool and emerging as a shining white bird. Surprised by this, he moved towards the pool and took a dip while holding onto a branch of the ber tree. Surprisingly, his whole body was cured immediately. On her return, Bibi Rajni was surprised to see her husband completely cured. She refused to believe the curing property of the miracle water. So, both Bibi Rajni and her husband visited Sikh Guru Ramdass, who took them to the pool again and proved the miracle of the water. A tank was built around the pool and it became famous for its miraculous healing power. The ber tree on its bank became known as Dukhbhanjani beri or sorrow-removing tree.

Usage

The leaves of the ber tree are used as fodder. The leaves are fed to tussar silk worms. The fruits are edible. The fruit can be eaten fresh and made into puddings, cakes, breads, jellies, soups, etc. In southern India, fresh or dried fruits (after removal of the seed) are pounded with tamarind, red chillies, salt and jaggery and dried under the sun to make cakes known as *ilanthai vadai* (in Tamil) or *ragi vadiyalu* (in Telugu). The fruits can be used as a coffee substitute. It can be grown as a hedge. Its wood is used for turnery, agricultural implements, fuel and charcoal. Lac is produced on its branches. The thorny branches are used for fence. The bark is a source of tannin. In addition to its traditional uses, the ber tree is used as a source of income through honey production, bee-keeping, etc.

The leaves of this tree are believed to promote hair growth. The fruit is used to gain weight, to improve muscular strength and to increase stamina. In Chinese medicine, the ber fruit is used to strengthen liver function. The dried fruits are used to treat chronic fatigue, diarrhoea, bronchitis, anaemia, etc. The seeds are used to treat insomnia, nervous exhaustion, night sweats and excessive perspiration. The root is used to treat dyspepsia. A decoction made out of the root is used to treat fever. The powder of the root is applied on old wounds and ulcers. The fruit and its seeds are used in Chinese and Korean traditional medicine to treat stress.

Cultivation Practices

The seeds are to be treated with concentrated sulphuric acid for 45 minutes for better germination. The seeds are to be dibbled in the nursery bed at 5 cm apart. Seedlings with four leaves can be transplanted into containers. Six-month-old saplings can be planted with a spacing of 3 m × 3 m in 30 cc pits. This is fast-growing and quick to mature. The seed-origin trees will yield fruits in 3–4 years. The tree responds well to coppicing. Over 400 cultivars have been selected. The major cultivars of the ber tree in India are *umran, banarsi karaka, kakrola, gola, mundia murhara, sanori, illaichi, safeda selected, kaithali, reshmi, chhuhara* and *seb*.

Acknowledgments

I am very thankful to Dr C.K. Sreedharan, IFS, former Principal Chief Conservator of Forests & Head of Forest Force (PCCF & HoFF), Chennai, for his valuable foreword to this book. I also express my sincere thanks to K.R. Varatharajan, IFS, former Deputy Conservator of Forests, and Dr K.K. Natarajan, former Dean, Saraswathy Narayanan College, Madurai for making necessary corrections. I also express my sincere gratitude to my son S. Praveen Kumar for his technical guidance. Finally, I may fail in my duty if I don't mention my life partner, Johnsi Rani, who rendered all possible support for writing this book.

I sincerely thank Assistant Commissioning Editor Priya Talwar for establishing a liaison and helping me in bringing out this book successfully. I acknowledge my debt to Rupa Publications, New Delhi, for providing me the great opportunity of writing this book.

Glossary

agamas: Sanskrit word meaning 'traditional doctrines'

arthropods: invertebrate animals with an exoskeleton, a segmented body and jointed appendages

birdlime: a sticky substance spread onto twigs to trap small birds

coppice: the new shoots that emerge when matured trees are cut

diuretic: causing increased passing of urine

drupe: a fleshy fruit with a thin skin and a central stone containing the seed

dysmenorrhoea: painful menstruation, typically involving abdominal cramps

ellipsoid: symmetrical about three mutually perpendicular axes that intersect at the centre

endemic: confined to a certain area

epiphyte: a plant growing on, but not nourished by another plant

glabrous: without hair

globose: almost spherical

gonorrhoea: a venereal disease involving inflammatory discharge from the urethra or vagina

haustoria: sucking roots of parasites

inflorescence: collection of flowers on a stem

lumbago: pain in the muscles and joints of the lower back

leucorrhoea: a whitish or yellowish discharge of mucus from the vagina

ophthalmia: inflammation of the eye, especially conjunctivitis

orchitis: inflammation of one or both of the testicles

pericarp: fruit wall

receptacle: the axis (stem) to which the floral organs are attached

ser: a traditional unit of mass and volume measurement that was used in large parts of Asia

spermatorrhoea: excessive, involuntary ejaculation

Bibliography

Ali, Salim, *The Book of Indian Birds*, Bombay Natural History Society, Mumbai, 1996.

Deane, Green, 'Monkey's Apple, Mimusops coriacea', *Eat the Weeds*, https://tinyurl.com/39jy7xjj. Accessed on 12 July 2023.

ENVIS Centre on Conservation of Ecological Heritage and Sacred Sites of India, https://tinyurl.com/5ch8p9dh. Accessed on 2 August 2023.

Flowers of India, https://tinyurl.com/bdf7f8ur. Accessed on 12 July 2023.

Gandhi, Maneka, and Yasmin Singh, *Brahma's Hair: On the Mythology of Indian Plants*, Rupa & Co., 2000.

Gupta, Shakti M., *Plant Myths and Traditions in India,* E.J. Brill, Leiden, 1971.

India Biodiversity Portal, https://tinyurl.com/jd6u2bdx. Accessed on 12 July 2023.

Jain, R, et al., 'A Review On Medicinal Importance Of Emblica Officinalis', *International Journal of Pharmaceutical Sciences and Research*, Vol. 6, No. 1, 2015, https://tinyurl.com/4sbw4wpa. Accessed on 2 August 2023.

Jain, V. '*Bombax Ceiba* Linn.: As an Umbrella Tree Species in Forests of Southern Rajasthan, India', *Research Journal of Environmental Sciences*, Vol. 5, No. 8, https://tinyurl.com/vp3vrru9. Accessed on 2 August 2023.

Joseph, S. John, and V. Sundararaju, 'Management Plan for Mudumalai Wildlife Sanctuary', Tamil Nadu Forest Department, Chennai, 1978.

Mani, P.S., *Valam Tharum Marangal Volumes 1-5*, New Century Book House, Chennai, 1992.

Matthew, K.M., *The Flora of the Palni Hills, South India*, The Rapinat Herbarium, St Joseph's College, Tiruchirappalli, 1999.

Mukherjee, Sugato, 'The Bishnoi: India's First Environmentalists', *The Diplomat*, 8 August 2019, https://tinyurl.com/h76v3puv. Accessed on 12 July 2023.

Orwa, C., et al., 'Agroforestree Database: A Tree Reference and Selection Guide Version 4.0', *World Agroforestry,* World Agroforestry Centre, 2009, https://tinyurl.com/5xdzv6hk. Accessed on 12 July 2023.

Pal, Sanchari, 'Food for Thought: Unpeeling the Mango's Interesting History in India', *The Better India*, 7 June 2016, https://tinyurl.com/4d6e8pa9. Accessed on 12 July 2023.

Panchavarnam, R., *Pirabanjamum Thaavarangalum*, Thaavara Thagaval Mayam, Panruti, 2011.

——, *Kabilarin Kurinjippaattu Thaavarangal*, Thaavara Thagaval Mayam, Panruti, 2011.

——, *Tholkaappiyarin Tholkaappiya Thaavarangal*, Thaavara Thagaval Mayam, Panruti, 2011.

Planet Ayurveda: Holistic Healing through Herbs, https://tinyurl.com/5n6rked7. Accessed on 12 July 2023.

Prabhala, Lakshmi, 'In Telangana's Interiors, the Mahua Tree Remains Sacred, Even as Demand for Its Flowers Decreases', *Firstpost*, 2 April 2018, https://tinyurl.com/8hctbddz. Accessed on 12 July 2023.

Rajasekharan, S., et al., *Stars and Trees- The Trees of the Nakshatravanam*, Tropical Botanic Garden and Research Institute, Thiruvananthapuram, 2005.

Ramachander, P.R., 'Lalitha Sahasranamam', Joshi, Yogesh and Krishna Maheshwari (trans.), *Hindupedia: The Hindu Encyclopedia,* https://tinyurl.com/2264nhra. Accessed on 12 July 2023.

Ravikumar, K., et al., *100 Red-Listed Medicinal Plants*, Foundation for Revitalisation of Local Health Traditions (FRLHT), Bangalore, 2000.

Sharma, Prabodh Chander, et al., 'A Review on Bael Tree', *Natural Product Radiance*, Vol. 6, No. 2, 2007.

Singh, A.K., Sanjay Singh, and P.L. Saroj, 'The Bael (Production Technology)', Technical Bulletin No. CIAH/Tech./Pub. No. 67, Director ICAR-CIAH, Bikaner.

Somasundaram, T.R., *A Handbook on the Identification and Description of Trees, Shrubs and Some Important Herbs of the Forests of the Southern States for the Use of the Southern Forest Rangers College, Coimbatore*, Southern Forest Rangers College, Coimbatore, 1963.

Strong, J. S., *The Legend of King Ashoka*, Princeton University Press, New York, 1983, p. 99.

Sundararaju, V., 'Management Plan for Kanyakumari Wildlife Sanctuary', Tamil Nadu Forest department, Chennai, 2007.

———, *Ecological Harmony*, Notion Press, Chennai, 2020.

———, *Jungle Chronicles*, Notion Press, Chennai, 2017.

———, *Maram Manitharin Nanban*, Valvil Printers, Tiruchirappalli, 2004.

'Surya's Tapestry: Ancient Rishis' Pathways to Hinduism', *Hindu Wisdom*, https://tinyurl.com/ynypr9ew. Accessed on 12 July 2023.

TopTropicals, https://tinyurl.com/24j39a34. Accessed on 12 July 2023.

Useful Tropical Plants Database, https://tinyurl.com/26m6tvy4. Accessed on 12 July 2023.

Walter, Kurt J., 'Sacred Trees Among the Tamil People of South India', *Suomen Antropologi: Journal of the Finnish Anthropological Society*, Vol. 40, No. 1, 2015.

Yoganarasimhan, S.N., and V. Chelladurai, *Medicinal Plants of India: Tamil Nadu, Volume 2*, Cyber Media, Bangalore, 2000.